THE ENTREPRENEUR'S PLAYBOOK ™

STARTUP YOUR DREAM BUSINESS

By: **STEVE CHONG**

Author, Speaker, Coach & Consultant

www.entrepreneursplaybook.com

THE ENTREPRENEUR'S PLAYBOOK:
HOW TO STARTUP YOUR DREAM BUSINESS

ISBN: 978-0-9858523-9-9

www.entrepreneursplaybook.com

Imagination is more important than knowledge.

~ Albert Einstein

Dear Future Entrepreneur,

Congratulations on the special purchase of your very own copy of **The ENTREPRENEUR'S PLAYBOOK**! *In your hands is everything you need to manifest your dream life into reality.*

This business startup guide was lovingly created to show you play-by-play the **ABC's of ENTREPRENEURSHIP**. It is inspired by our belief that *anyone* - regardless of their background, age, experience or education level - can live the ***Real American Dream of Business Ownership***.

Becoming an entrepreneur is an incredibly phenomenal journey of *self-discovery* and *sacrifice*. Our mission is to help you capture your business dreams from the initial spark of creative inspiration to the development of your **BIG IDEA** to the ultimate delivery of your company's goods and services.

It is said, the best opportunities in life are the ones we create from the heart. Look around, everyday people are waking up to the epiphany that they can profit from their passion and build their labor of love. With owning your own enterprise, you can enjoy a lifetime of income, true job security and have the ***REAL TIME of YOUR LIFE.***

Thank you for your business!

In Freedom,

STEVE CHONG

Author of The Entrepreneur's Playbook

TABLE OF CONTENTS

FOREWORD

INTRODUCTION 1
What is Entrepreneurship, Exactly? 6
Do You Really Have What It Takes? 11
How Do I Use This Playbook? 17

STEP 1: **BREAK THE RULES** 23
A. Dreaming Your Business Vision 25
B. Designing Your Business Mission 32
C. Developing Your Business Strategies 39

STEP 2: **KNOW THY CUSTOMER** 47
A. Researching Your Marketplace 49
B. Marketing Your Company 56
C. Selling Your Goods 63

STEP 3: **GET IT ORGANIZED** 71
A. Establishing Your Brand 73
B. Capitalizing Your Venture 80
C. Forming Your Organization 87

STEP 4: **CRAFT A BUSINESS PLAN** 95
A. Developing Your Marketing Strategy 97
B. Establishing Your Operational Framework 104
C. Mapping Out Your Financial Roadmap 111

STEP 5: **PROMOTE YOUR BRAND** 119
A. Producing Your Sales Arsenal 121
B. Coordinating Your Marketing & Sales 128
C. Growing Your Business Network 135

STEP 6: **CHIEF YOUR OPERATIONS** 143
A. Governing Your Enterprise 145
B. Monitoring Your Communications 152
C. Controlling Your Finances 159

GLOSSARY OF TERMS 167

This is a self-initiation into the world of the entrepreneur.

DREAMING THE FUTURE

NO DOUBT that if you are reading this **RIGHT NOW**, it is your **HEART'S DESIRE** to launch your **DREAM BUSINESS** and live the life of a **SUCCESSFUL ENTREPRENEUR**.

This is your invitation to awaken the vision that lives within you... and begin shaping it into reality. This is where your entrepreneurial journey begins.

IMAGINE IT NOW in full technicolor, depth and dimension. You now hold the playbook. Now it is time to activate it - with your mind's eye, your heart's emotion and your body's devotion.

See it.

Feel it.

Action it into being.

IF YOU CAN DREAM IT, YOU CAN DO IT!
Claim your visions. Write it with power, boldness and clarity.

Use the space below to capture and crystallize your **Grand Vision**: the meaningful impact you will create, the core values that will guide you and the lasting legacy you will build.

Before you begin, pause.
Center your breath.
Now, begin to dream with your whole being.

Visualize the answers to the following prompts as scenes already happening in your future:

IMAGINE:
You have been teleported into your dream future.
What Would You Attempt If You Knew You Could Not Fail?

IMAGINE:
You are the founder of a thriving company.
What If Time, Money and Resources Were Not Limiting Factors.

IMAGINE:
You wake up each day inspired and energized.
What If Your Deepest Life Passion Became Your Business?

IMAGINE:
Your dream life and waking life merging.
What If Your Life Passion Became Your Business?

UNVEILING THE ENTREPRENEURIAL BLUEPRINT
Every vision begins with belief and becomes real through action.

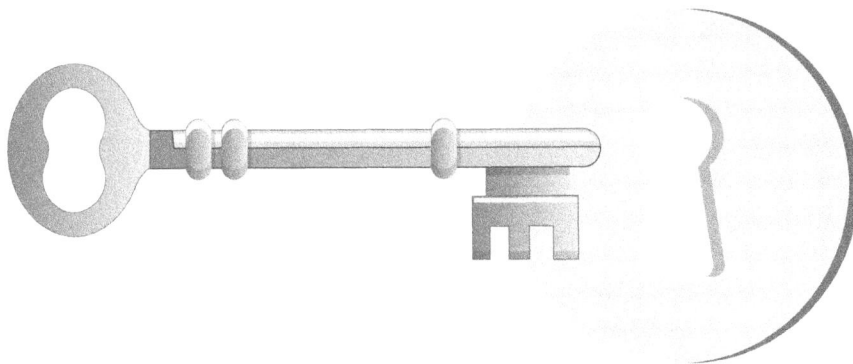

CAN YOU SEE IT? - IN YOUR MIND'S EYE
Your Mind is the Crucible Where Intention Makes Anything Possible.

Vividly picture your most passionate dreams coming into a clear vision, visualize every single detail, noticing what is around you and who is with you.

CAN YOU FEEL IT? - IN YOUR HEART OF HEARTS
Your Heart is the Furnance Where Passion Ignites Unstoppable Drive.

Deeply feel your burning passion fueling unwavering drive, embracing every emotion, sensing the fire within, and connecting with your purpose.

CAN YOU EXECUTE IT? - WITH YOU HANDS AND FEET
Your Body is the Forge Where Action Crafts Enduring Triumph.

Resolutely act to shape your vision into reality, molding every step, seizing each moment and building your legacy with unrelenting resolve.

Between execution and being exists the sacred ground of becoming.

YOU ARE THE CREATOR!
Entrepreneurship opens the door to infinite possibilities.

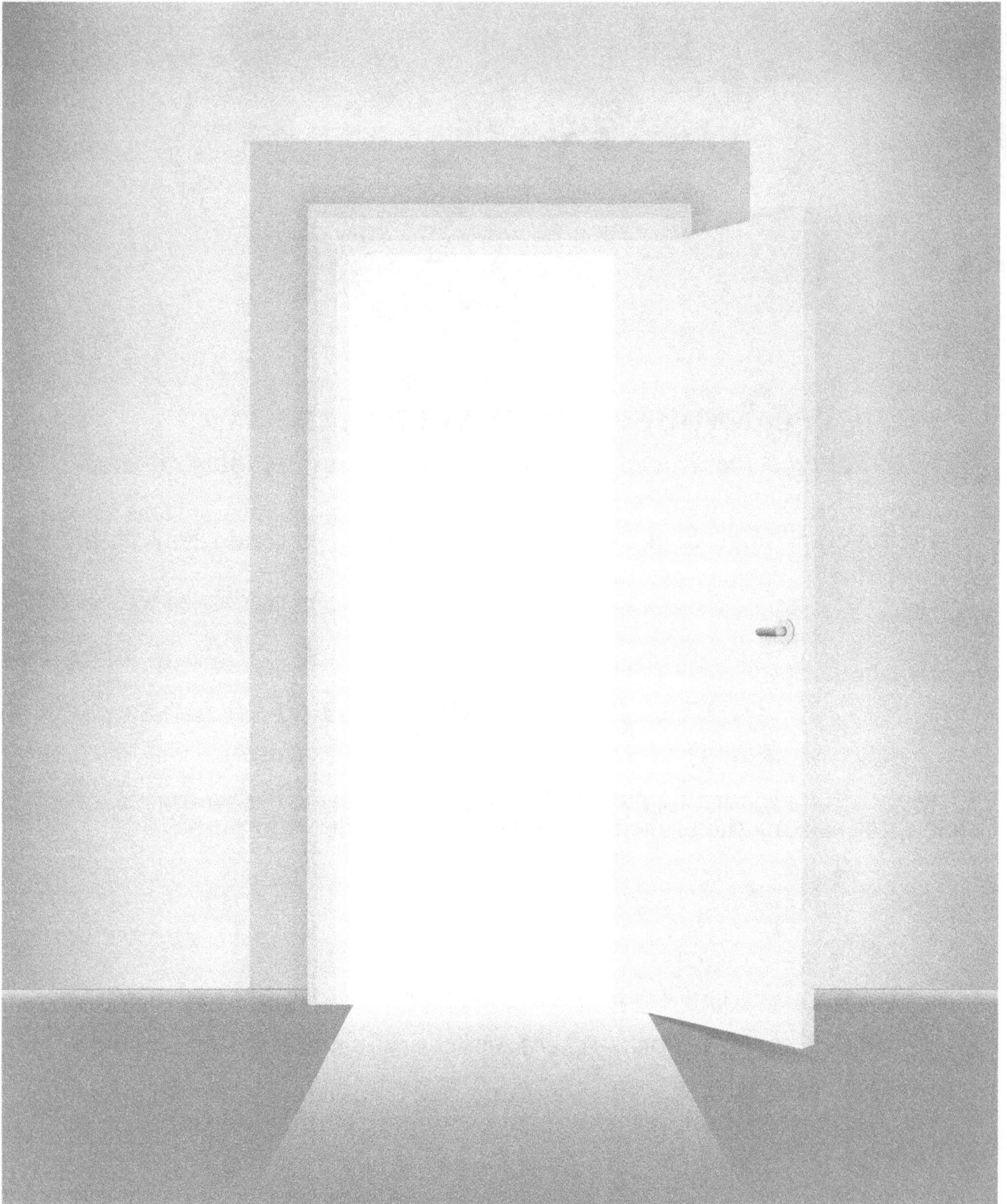

Dream Big. Start Small. Act Now.

This Introductory Chapter Answers
the Following 3 Questions:

WHAT IS ENTREPRENEURSHIP, EXACTLY?

DO YOU HAVE WHAT IT TAKES?

HOW DO I USE THIS PLAYBOOK?

WHAT IS ENTREPRENEURSHIP, EXACTLY?
In a word, Entrepreneurship is FREEDOM.

Entrepreneurship can be symbolized into to a cube - each of its six sides representing a distinct dimension of real freedom.

Freedom to:
LIVE YOUR PASSION

Freedom to:
BE YOUR OWN BOSS

Freedom to:
CREATE TRUE JOB SECURITY

Freedom to:
SET YOUR OWN SCHEDULES

Freedom to:
EARN MONEY INDEPENDENCE

Freedom to:
HAVE FUN AND BE FREE!

These interconnected planes: form a multidimensional framework for you to build a life and business that reflect your true aspirations.

Freedom To:
LIVE YOUR PASSION

Successful entrepreneurs are motivated by far more than financial gain and material wealth - they are guided by their hearts, seeking genuine happiness, fulfillment and and a life where every day aligns with their soul's purpose.

When you are sincerely passionate about what you do, you naturally give it your all, investing your precious energy, creativity and spirit into every single endeavor.

Authentic passion fuels enduring triumph, transforming obstacles into stepping stones. Living your passion wholeheartedly transcends building a business - it is about claiming sovereignty over your time, energy and joy - where work is about shaping a life you truly love.

Does your current entrepreneurial journey ignite the same joy and purpose as your dreams demand?

Freedom To:
BE YOUR OWN BOSS

Taking ownership of your path means stepping into the role of conscious creator, not just spectator. With self-employment, you gain the sacred autonomy to make decisions that reflect your purest vision, values and awakened strengths - crafting reality of your own design.

Embracing this freedom empowers you to make decisions that vibrantly align with your vision, cultivate growth, and create opportunities. It's through this autonomy that you transform challenges into triumphs, shaping your future on your own terms.

You are not just building a business, you are in fact designing a life of independence, empowerment and limitless possibility, where every success is a direct result of your choices and leadership.

Are you playing life on your own terms or still following someone else's rules?

Freedom To:
CREATE TRUE JOB SECURITY

In the past, working for an employer and depending on them to take care of you represented job security. Today, job security comes from within and by building a successful business.

By taking control of your career and financial future, you create your own security, ensuring long-term growth and stability. Entrepreneurship empowers you to navigate uncertainty and turn challenges into opportunities for success.

Entrepreneurship transforms uncertainty into opportunity, empowering you to weather change and create lasting value. When you build your own business, you do not just secure a job, you create a foundation of stability, freedom and lasting success that is all yours.

Does your security reside in someone else's system or your ability to create opportunity from uncertainty?

Freedom To:
SET YOUR OWN SCHEDULES

When you work for yourself, you gain the flexibility to decide when, how and with whom you work. This autonomy allows you to legitimately own your time, blending work and life in a way that supports both productivity and personal well-being.

You have the power to bring your ideas to life on your schedule, not someone else's. Entrepreneurship enables you to design a lifestyle that accurately reflects your passions, values and priorities, making every day more meaningful, rewarding and uniquely yours.

By mastering your schedule, you are not just managing time - you are creating a life where freedom, balance and success flourish on your terms, allowing you to thrive in every area and savor every moment.

Does your current schedule reflect your priorities or someone else's?

Freedom To:
EARN MONEY INDEPENDENCE

Entrepreneurial ownership unleashes unlimited earning potential, transcending traditional salary constraints. Exchanging your time for predetermined compensation represents perpetual limitation.

When you architect your enterprise, your wealth creation capacity depends exclusively on your vision, execution excellence and entrepreneurial determination. Launching your venture empowers you to definitively escape cyclical financial dependency, securing mastery over your economic trajectory.

Authentic financial sovereignty transcends mere income generation - it means building a legacy where your strategic efforts unlock endless opportunities and lasting prosperity.

Does your income reflect what you are worth or what someone else decided you are worth?

Freedom To:
HAVE FUN AND BE FREE!

Authentic entrepreneurship is about blurring the line between work and play - between vocation and passion. Time to take that leap of faith, embrace risk, set parameters, define objectives and manifest aspirations.

When you master timeless entrepreneurial principles, work transforms into an engine of exhilaration, innovation and profound personal realization. You are no longer confined by rigid rules or expectations - instead, you design a life where passion fuels productivity and freedom drives success.

By turning your work into play, you create a life where success feels effortless and freedom becomes your greatest reward.

Does your work feel more like obligation or adventure and which would your most authentic self choose?

As you rotate this cube of freedom with your mind's eye, tracing each of its six faces, you grasp the truth: entrepreneurship transcends career - it is in essence, the metamorphosis of your very existence.

Vision, risk, innovation, resilience, leadership and impact converge in this prism, each facet a compass point toward a legacy aligned with your highest intentions.

Here, at the intersection of skill and soul, your daily work becomes sacred craft - your labor of love.

This is sovereignty over destiny - the personal liberty to architect life and enterprise as one, unlocking the potential to create, lead and manifest your innermost and most noble values.

Entrepreneurship is not just a career path, it is the alchemy of turning vision into legacy, where every obstacle becomes the path for your masterpiece.

DO YOU REALLY HAVE WHAT IT TAKES?
In a word, Entrepreneurship demands RESILIENCE.

An entrepreneur's journey can be envisioned as a pyramid, its eight edges representing the key traits of a successful entrepreneur

PASSION:
Intense Enthusiasm. Purposeful Devotion. Unyielding Determination.

LEADERSHIP:
Visionary Command. Empowering Influence. Resolute Adaptability.

CREATIVITY:
Imaginative Spark. Resourceful Ingenuity. Curios Exploration.

COMMUNICATION SKILLS:
Persuasive Clarity. Empathetic Connection Storytelling Magnetism.

INTEGRITY:
Unwavering Honesty. Moral Courage. Consistent Authenticity.

INTUITION:
Instinctive Insight. Empathic Discernment. Visceral Acumen.

COMMITMENT:
Steadfast Resolve. Sacrificial Dedication. Enduing Loyalty.

PATIENCE:
Strategic Restraint. Resilient Endurance. Nurturing Foresight.

If you believe that you can embody a majority of these 8 essential attributes and characteristics above, you may have the mindset of the entrepreneur.

Do You Have?
PASSION

First and foremost, exceptional entrepreneurs engage in their labor of love and immerse themselves in their most passionate pursuits. They are fiercely self-motivated, never needing external pressure to be accountable, efficient or productive.

They channel this relentless drive into cultivating a company vision, mission and strategy that seamlessly aligns their personal dreams with their customers' needs, building a brand that inspires unwavering loyalty, trust and genuine connection.

Do you have a clear, crystallized vision of your business that resonates with your purpose that keeps you motivated to overcome the inevitable challenges along your journey?

Do You Have?
CREATIVITY

Successful entrepreneurs are crafty like busy beavers, always enterprising in thought and willing to do whatever it takes to deliver the goods, products and services that their target markets truly want, need and desire - in the right timing.

They harness the power of innovative market research and deep customer insights, translating creativity into clear, actionable strategies that set their solutions apart and provide exceptional value. This pursuit of originality fuels their ability to adapt, evolve and stay ahead of the curve.

Can you consistently think outside the box of conventional boundaries and devise breakthrough solutions to meet the ever-evolving needs of your target market?

Do You Have?
INTEGRITY

Authenticity and transparency are the foundations of lasting entrepreneurial success, influencing every decision and relationship you build. Entrepreneurs who embody integrity honor the laws of karma, practice the Golden Rule and uphold a steadfast personal and professional Code of Ethics in all aspects of life and business.

This unwavering moral compass fosters deep trust, allowing them to form enduring partnerships and create a workplace culture where ethical practices drive both profitability and true collaboration.

Are your daily business decisions consistently guided by integrity, building trust and nurturing ethical relationships with customers, partners and team members?

Do You Have?:
COMMITMENT

Commitment in entrepreneurship means embracing your business as a dedicated 24/7/365 lifestyle, not just a job. It requires unwavering daily focus, indomitable perseverance and a drive for excellence in every aspect of execution.

Entrepreneurs who are truly committed approach their journey with strategic planning, leveraging strong operational processes and a mindset of continuous improvement to turn obstacles into opportunities for sustainable growth.

Are you ready to devote the time, energy and relentless focus required to build your business as a lifelong pursuit - demanding your full commitment, daily?

Do You Have?
LEADERSHIP

Leadership in entrepreneurship means taking full ownership of your company's vision, direction and outcomes. True leaders are goal-oriented and proactive, seizing opportunities while skillfully managing risk to drive sustainable growth.

They empower their teams by setting clear benchmarks and refining organizational structures to translate vision into decisive action. By inspiring innovation and resilience at every level, entrepreneurial leaders create an environment where everyone can thrive.

Can you motivate and guide your team while embracing responsibility for your business's success and navigating challenges with confidence and clarity?

Do You Have?:
COMMUNICATIONS SKILLS

Mastering communication skills is essential for every entrepreneur, shaping how you connect, persuade and lead in a competitive marketplace. Exceptional communicators craft compelling messages, actively listen, and use both verbal and nonverbal cues to build trust and rapport with their audience.

Through clear storytelling, omnichannel strategies and genuine engagement, they amplify brand equity and transform prospects into loyal advocates.

Can you consistently deliver persuasive messages, listen deeply, and foster meaningful connections that elevate your brand and fuel lasting business growth?

Do You Have?
INTUITION

Intuition, other kwown as the sixth sense, is a powerful asset for entrepreneurs, guiding decision-making when logic alone is not enough. Those who excel in business trust their instincts and inner voice, allowing them to sense opportunities and navigate uncertainty with confidence.

By blending intuitive insight with data analytics, they anticipate market trends and make well-informed choices. This balance between gut feeling and hard evidence empowers bold, timely action that keeps businesses agile and ahead of the curve.

Do you trust your intuition and can you integrate it with concrete data to make courageous, forward-thinking decisions for your business?

Do You Have?:
PATIENCE

Patience is the quiet strength that underpins every lasting entrepreneurial journey, reminding us that building something meaningful takes time, vigilance, and continuous dedication to our craft.

Entrepreneurs who practice patience adapt to evolving challenges, maintain focus on long-term goals and invest in relationships that secure their company's position in the market.

Can you maintain your focus on the bigger picture, navigate inevitable setbacks and keep improving your business, knowing that enduring achievement is built moment by moment over time?

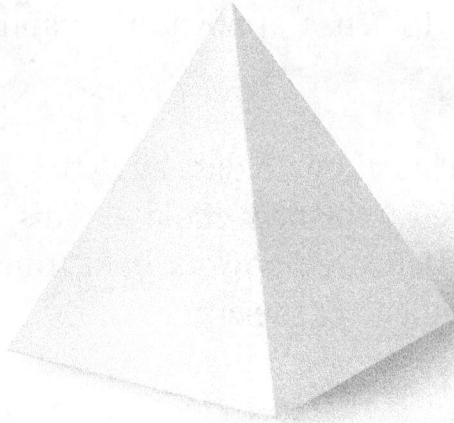

If you have none or just a few of these core attributes and characteristics, self-employment would seem like the wrong career choice. However, do not be discouraged if you do no't possess all of these traits right away. Entrepreneurship is a journey of growth, learning and adaptation.

Many successful entrepreneurs have started with limited attributes but built them over time through experience, perseverance and continuous self-improvement.

If you are committed to cultivating the mindset and skills necessary for success, there is always room for transformation.

The key is to remain open, adaptable and willing to embrace change as you build your entrepreneurial path.

The question is not whether you have what it takes, it is whether you are willing to become the kind of person who does.

HOW DO I USE THIS PLAYBOOK?
Welcome to the art, science and magic of ENTREPRENEURSHIP.

Picture this playbook as a sphere with six dynamic orbits guiding your entrepreneurial ascent through six key steps.

Step 1:
BREAK THE RULES

Step 2:
KNOW THY CUSTOMER

Step 3:
GET IT ORGANIZED

Step 4:
CRAFT A BUSINESS PLAN

Step 5:
PROMOTE YOUR BRAND

Step 6:
CHIEF YOUR OPERATIONS

Each step is anchored by the vital questions and key tactics to action your ideas into reality and unlock your dreams into fruition.

Step 1:
BREAK THE RULES

Within Step 1's Triple Play—Dreaming Your Vision, Designing Your Mission, and Developing Your Strategies—you will define your aspirations, clarify your purpose and craft actionable plans to bring your entrepreneurial dream to life.

This step ignites your mind's crucible, heart's furnace and hands' forge, sculpting a multifaceted destiny from passion's raw essence and transforming ideas into tangible momentum. By integrating your vision, mission and strategies, you establish a resilient framework that guides your journey from inspiration to realization ensuring every step is purposeful and aligned.

Step 1 empowers you to shatter conventions, forging an unbreakable foundation for your entrepreneurial odyssey and setting the stage for lasting impact and growth.

Step 2:
KNOW THY CUSTOMER

Within Step 2's Triple Play—Establishing Your Marketplace, Marketing Your Company, and Selling Your Goods—you will gain clarity on who your ideal customers are, understand their needs, and build strategies to effectively connect, engage and deliver value to them.

This strategic trinity kindles your mind's crucible to discern customer desires, your heart's furnace to forge authentic connections, and your hands' forge to craft compelling value, weaving a multifaceted tapestry of impact.

Step 2 aligns marketplace insight, marketing finesse and sales mastery to create a vibrant ecosystem that resonates with your entrepreneurial vision empowering you to truly know, serve and inspire your customers.

Step 3:
GET IT ORGANIZED

Within Step 3's Triple Play—Establishing Your Business Identity, Capitalizing Your Business Venture, and Forming Your Business Organization—you will lay the groundwork to structure and organize your operations, secure the necessary resources and set up systems that drive efficiency and growth.

This strategic trinity sparks your mind's crucible to craft a distinctive identity, your heart's furnace to fuel resourceful ambition and your hands' forge to build robust systems, weaving a solid foundation of entrepreneurial triumph.

Step 3's Triple Play emboldens you to defy chaos, rise above uncertainty, sculpting a cornerstone for your enterprise's transcendent ascent and empowering you to lead with clarity, confidence, and purpose.

Step 4:
CRAFT A BUSINESS PLAN

Within Step 4's Triple Play—Developing Your Marketing Strategy, Establishing Your Operational Framework, and Controlling Your Finances—you will develop a structured business plan that integrates your marketing, operations, and financial strategies to ensure clarity and actionable steps for growth.

This strategic trinity kindles your mind's crucible to devise strategic clarity, your heart's furnace to infuse plans with passionate purpose, and your hands' forge to craft a blueprint of enduring success, cultivating a legacy of success that stands the test of time.

Step 4's Triple Play emboldens you to rise above mediocrity, sculpting an indomitable roadmap and empowering your enterprise for extraordinary victory.

Step 5:
PROMOTE YOUR BRAND

Within Step 5s Triple Play—Producing Your Sales Materials, Coordinating Marketing & Sales, and Growing Your Business Network—you'll craft compelling sales materials, optimize marketing strategies, and expand your network, ensuring all efforts are aligned to attract customers and drive sustainable business growth.

This strategic trinity ignites your mind's crucible to design persuasive narratives, your heart's furnace to forge authentic influence, and your hands' forge to cultivate expansive, lasting connections, weaving a multifaceted mosaic of entrepreneurial impact.

Step 5's Triple Play emboldens you to defy obscurity, sculpting an indomitable presence and elevating your enterprise for transcendent triumph.

Step 5:
CHIEF YOUR OPERATIONS

Within Step 6's Triple Play—Governing Your Vision, Monitoring Your Communications, and Controlling Your Finances—you will ensure your brand stays aligned with your goals, maintain clear communication, and manage finances to achieve sustainable growth and long-term success.

This strategic trinity ignites your mind's crucible to steer visionary alignment, your heart's furnace to foster authentic dialogue, and your hands' forge to sculpt financial resilience with disciplined focus, weaving a multifaceted legacy of entrepreneurial dominion.

Step 6's Triple Play emboldens you to defy instability, sculpting an unbreakable bastion for your enterprise's long-term legacy with enduring strength.

This playbook is built on a structured framework designed to alchemize your entrepreneurial dream into a thriving reality. Each layer of the hierarchy serves a unique purpose, guiding you from inspiration to manifestation:

Like a philosopher's stone transmuting lead into gold, this framework converts raw potential into disciplined mastery - one transformative step at a time.

It empowers you to move with intention, aligning your creative drive with strategic execution to build something both visionary and viable.

Consider these pages your philosopher's stone: where disciplined action transmutes "**What If**" into "**What Is**".

To use this Playbook effectively, start with Step 1: Break the Rules, where you will unlock the mindset, vision and strategies to boldly begin your entrepreneurial journey.

STEP 1:

BREAK THE RULES

"Your time is limited, so don't waste it living someone else's life."
~ Steve Jobs (Apple Founder)

In the GREAT GAME of BUSINESS and in LIFE, your TIME is your most precious commodity and unrenewable resource for it is the very currency of living.

For the entrepreneur, the saying rings true: TIME is MONEY. Invested wisely, incredible achievements in commerce can be realized. Time wasted - well, it is gone forever!

Entrepreneurship is not for those complacent with the status quo. It is for those brave enough to challenge the prevailing conventional wisdom, to question the accepted norms and to envision something better.

Do not be a part of the mindless throngs of the unthinking majority. Instead, harness the power of free enterprise and ignite your entrepreneurial spirit by launching the business of YOUR dreams - RIGHT NOW!

Ultimately, breaking the rules is more than a mere strategy, it is the essential mindset of entrepreneurial transformation. You must embrace risk and innovate to pursue your vision with relentless determination, no matter the obstacles.

Remember that:
History's most revolutionary achievements have emerged from visionaries courageous enough to challenge longstanding conventions.

This is not about following someone else's blueprint, it is about mapping your Grand Vision and dreamweaving your own unique path to success.

To actualize this potential, you must first liberate yourself from the constraints that confine countless entrepreneurs.

Trust your intuition, defy the ordinary and then proceed to manifest something spectacular that only you can birth as your brainchild.

This is the key moment you stop waiting for permission and take full charge of your destiny.

This is where it all begins.

ISN'T IT TIME TO BREAK THE RULES OF CONVENTIONAL THINKING AND GO INTO BUSINESS FOR YOURSELF?

BREAK THE RULES

TRIPLE PLAY STRATEGY

Ⓐ

DREAMING YOUR BUSINESS VISION
What Is Your Company's Ultimate Aspiration?

Envision My Core Passions

Envision My Core Customers

Envision My Core Strengths

Envision My Core Impacts

Ⓑ

DESIGNING YOUR BUSINESS MISSION
What Is the Purpose of Your Business?

Define My Core Purpose

Define My Core Advantages

Define My Core Values

Define My Core Principles

Ⓒ

DEVELOPING YOUR BUSINESS STRATEGIES
How Will You Actualize Your Business?

Construct My Core Goals

Construct My Core Objectives

Construct My Core Timelines

Construct My Core Metrics

ISN'T IT TIME TO BREAK THE RULES OF CONVENTIONAL THINKING AND GO INTO BUSINESS FOR YOURSELF?

DREAMING YOUR BUSINESS VISION
What Is Your Company's Ultimate Aspiration?

Envision My Core Passions

What Inspirations Ignite Your Entrepreneurial Spirit?

Identify the foundational motivators that fuel your heartfelt desire to pioneer a bold, new and original venture.

Envision My Core Customers

Who Will Purchase Your Company's Goods?

Identify the specific individuals your business exists to serve and inspire by understanding their needs, dreams and challenges.

Envision My Core Strengths

What Is Your Special Offering to the Market?

Identify the distinctive talents, capabilities and skills you bring to the marketplace that define your value and set you apart.

Envision My Core Impacts

What Enduring Difference Will Your Business Make?

Identify the legacy you want to create that will reshape your industry and leave a lasting mark on the lives you serve.

By ***Dreaming Your Business Vision***, you now the architect designing the blueprint of your enterprise's aspirational trajectory, establishing the foundational cornerstone for succeeding development with clarity and conviction.

ENVISION MY CORE PASSIONS

What Inspirations Ignite Your Entrepreneurial Spirit?

Right now: You are identifying the foundational motivators that fuel your heartfelt desire to pioneer a bold, new and original venture.

🔻 KEY TAKEAWAY

Recognize that: Your Core Passions serve to fuel unwavering motivation, align your business with your fundamental interests and drive long-term success by fostering a sense of purpose. Envisioning what truly activates your entrepreneurial spirit harmonizes your vision with your authentic passions.

🔓 KEY ACTION

Outline: Start by detailing your innate motivations to create the foundation for both profitable enterprise and personal fulfillment. Execute by channeling these passions into purpose-driven strategies that address genuine market needs, ensuring your business resonates authentically and impactfully.

✏️ KEY NOTES

ENVISION MY CORE CUSTOMERS

Who Will Purchase Your Company's Goods?

Right now: You are identifying the specific individuals your business exists to serve and inspire by understanding their needs, dreams and challenges.

🔻 KEY TAKEAWAY

Recognize that: Your Core Customers serve to shape targeted marketing efforts, drive engagement and boost sales while building lasting brand loyalty through relevance and connection. Envisioning the prime audience can unlock the ability to deliver solutions that precisely meet their needs.

🔓 KEY ACTION

Outline: Start by detailing your core customers' defining demographics to build a foundation for precise targeting and impactful engagement. Execute by researching their motivations, psychographics and behavioral patterns to develop detailed profiles that elevate marketing effectiveness.

✏️ KEY NOTES

ENVISION MY CORE STRENGTHS

What Is Your Special Offering to the Market?

Right now: You are identifying the distinctive talents, capabilities and skills you bring to the marketplace that define your value and set you apart.

KEY TAKEAWAY

Recognize that: Your Core Strengths serve to carve out a niche in the market, sharpen your competitive edge and attract loyal customers by delivering unique value. Envisioning these key differentiators empowers you to lead with purpose and scale your business with confidence.

KEY ACTION

Outline: Start by detailing how your leadership, skills and talents align with the needs of your target market. Execute by demonstrating how your unique abilities solve real problems, deliver measurable impact, and amplify the value your business provides to customers.

KEY NOTES

ENVISION MY CORE IMPACTS
What Enduring Difference Will Your Business Make?

Right now: You are identfiying the legacy you want your business to create that will reshape your industry and leave a lasting mark on the lives you serve.

KEY TAKEAWAY

Recognize that: Your Core Impacts serve to clarify the long-term significance of your work and inspires stakeholders to support a greater cause. Envisioning these key outcomes aligns daily actions with visionary outcomes and enhances your brand's credibility and trust.

KEY ACTION

Outline: Start by detailing your business's legacy by assessing its contributions to customers, communities, and the environment through the lens of impact and intention. Execute by setting goals that foster a positive ripple effect extending beyond profits.

KEY NOTES

DRAFTING MY COMPANY VISION STATEMENT
What Is My Company's Ultimate Aspiration?

Now, let us bring together your passions, audience, strengths and impact into a bold and inspiring declaration that captures your company's ultimate aspiration. A powerful vision inspires your team, partners and customers - uniting them under a shared aspiration that drives lasting motivation.

Outline a bold and aspirational vision statement by answering these four guiding questions:

What passion drives the heart of your business?
Identify the core motivation that fuels your commitment.

What unwavering beliefs guide every decision and action?
Define the non-negotiable ethical and cultural pillars that shape your operations.

What unique strengths/capabilities set your business apart?
Clarify what makes your approach effective and distinct.

What lasting change will you create in people's lives?
Articulate the measurable transformation or legacy your work will deliver.

DRAFTING MY COMPANY VISION STATEMENT

Capture the quintessence of what your organization seeks to become - its ultimate destination. Pursue precision, unwavering conviction and bold imagination as you crystallize the future only your vision can manifest.

Use the space below to architect your vision statement, drawing from your passions, ideal customer insights, distinctive competencies and aspirational impact. Employ concise declarations, convincing language and dynamic imagery to materialize your enterprise's future reality.

MY VISION STATEMENT DRAFT:

This is your space to write, refine and crystallize your company's ultimate aspiration.

Ⓑ

DESIGNING YOUR BUSINESS MISSION
What Is the Purpose of Your Business?

🔒 KEY TACTICS

Define My Core Purpose

Why Does Your Company Exist?

Identify the timeless reason for being, the core motivations that transcends what you sell or earn.

Define My Core Values

What Does Your Company Stand For?

Identify the central beliefs, principles and ethical code that will govern your daily business operations.

Define My Core Advantages

What Does Your Company Do Better Than the Competition?

Identify and amplify the unique strengths and competitive advantages that your business delivers better than anyone else.

Define My Core Principles

What Behaviors Guide How Your Business Operates Daily?

Identify how to turn core values into actionable standards that guide decisions, culture and operations.

By ***Designing Your Business Mission,*** you give your business its main reason for being in the marketplace. This central guiding light guides all operations, articulating core values that drive decisions and shape market identity.

DEFINE MY CORE PURPOSE

Why Does Your Company Exist?

Right Now: You are identifying the fundamental reasons for your business's existence - the deeper 'why' that transcends products, services or profits.

Recognize that: Your Core Purpose crystallizes your reason for being, fuels mission-driven operations and inspires stakeholders by anchoring your business in meaning beyond profit. Defining your core purpose clarifies your organization's driving force, securing mission alignment.

Outline: Start by detailing 3-5 of your company's foundational reasons for existing beyond financial success. Execute by articulating how these core motivations drive daily actions, inspire your team and shape the meaningful change you strive to achieve.

DEFINE MY CORE VALUES

What Does Your Company Stand For?

Right Now: You are identifying the central beliefs, principles and ethical code that will govern your daily business operations.

Recognize that: Your Core Values establish ethical boundaries, shape culture and build trust with stakeholders by reflecting what your business truly stands for. Defining your core values clarifies your company's identity and builds relationships with customers, employees and partners.

Outline: Start by detailing 3–5 bedrock principles that will define how your company operates and interacts. Execute by embedding these non-negotiable values into daily behaviors, decision-making processes and cultural norms to shape your company's identity and guide its direction.

DEFINE MY CORE ADVANTAGES

What Does Your Company Do Better Than the Competition?

Right Now: You are identifying and amplify the unique strengths and competitive advantages that your business delivers better than anyone else.

Recognize that: Your Core Advantages differentiate your business, attract ideal customers and build value by delivering benefits others cannot replicate. Defining these core advantages advances your strategic position, strengthens loyalty and increases your competitive resilience.

Outline: Start by detailing 3–5 of your company's most compelling differentiators that deliver unique value and competitive edge. Execute by conducting a SWOT analysis to identify strategic opportunities where these strengths can be leveraged for maximum market impact.

DEFINE MY CORE PRINCIPLES

What Behaviors Guide How Your Business Operates Daily?

Right Now: You are identifying how to turn core values into actionable standards that guide decisions, culture and operations.

Recognize that: Your Core Principles anchor your business in unwavering beliefs that guide decisions, shape culture and forge trust with all stakeholders. Defining these non-negotiable tenets align actions with purpose and ensures long-term value beyond fleeting trends.

Outline: Start by detailing 3–5 foundational beliefs that will guide your company's behaviors, policies and decisions. Execute by embedding these principles into daily operations and decision-making processes, ensuring they shape culture, influence actions and reinforce your brand identity.

DRAFTING MY COMPANY MISSION STATEMENT
What Is the Purpose of My Business?

A potent mission weaves your fundamental values, target audience insights, distinctive strengths and existential purpose into a unifying strategic mandate. An impactful Mission Statement ignites unwavering dedication and fuels day-to-day execution, creating seamless bridges between present tactical actions and visionary future aspirations.

Outline a clear and compelling mission statement by answering these four guiding questions:

What is your company's core purpose?
Why do you exist beyond making money? What essential human need or problem are you committed to addressing?

What values shape your behavior and decisions?
Define the principles that guide how your busin
ess shows up in the world - internally and externally.

What unique advantages set your company apart?
What do you do differently or better than others in your space - and why does it matter to those you serve?

What non-negotiable rules govern how you deliver value?
Define the ironclad standards that ensure consistency, quality and integrity in every customer interaction.

DRAFTING MY COMPANY MISSION STATEMENT

Capture the quintessence of why your organization exists - its fundamental motivating force. Pursue precision, authentic expression and strategic focus as you define the purpose only your mission can embody.

Use the space below to distill key mission insights, crafting structured statements to illuminate core commitments defining your organization's purpose. Employ concise language, authentic principles and operational clarity to shape your enterprise's foundational identity.

MY MISSION STATEMENT DRAFT:

This is your space to write down, refine and solidify your company's purpose.

DEVELOPING YOUR BUSINESS STRATEGIES
How Will You Actualize Your Business?

Construct My Core Goals

Where Do You See Your Company in 1, 3 and 5 Years?

Identify and set clear, measurable targets that align your vision with execution, to provide direction for your business.

Construct My Core Objectives

How Will You ReachYour Company's Goals?

Identify practical, sequential and actionable objectives that break down overarching key results into manageable steps.

Construct My Core Timelines

What Deadlines Have You Set For Each Company Goal?

Identify and establish a clear chronology for actualizing your business objectives and transformative milestones.

Construct My Core Metrics

How Will You Measure Your Success?

Identify and establish criteria, benchmarks and performance thresholds to assess progress and success.

By ***Developing Your Business Strategies***, you can channel your passionate life-force energy and direct your business venture toward tangible goals, fostering real-life outcomes that propel your commercial triumph with sustained momentum.

CONSTRUCT MY CORE GOALS

Where Do You See Your Company in 1, 3, and 5 Years?

Right Now: You are identifying and setting clear, achievable goals to provide direction for your business.

Recognize that: Your Core Goals offer a visionary roadmap, fueling ambition and aligning your team's energy toward tangible milestones. Constructing clear business goals, provides clarity and unity of purpose by mapping future growth across strategic time horizons.

Outline: Start by detailing your keystone ambitions across short, mid and long-term horizons using the SMART framework (Specific, Measurable, Achievable, Relevant, Time-bound). Execute by aligning your team around shared objectives to drive focused, measurable progress.

CONSTRUCT MY CORE OBJECTIVES

How Will You Reach Your Company's Goals?

Right Now: You are identifying the practical, actionable objectives that break down broad goals into manageable steps.

Recognize that: Your Core Objectives translate your company's high-level goals into precise, executable actions that fuel progress and performance. Constructing these objectives with clarity and alignment ensures that every initiative contributes meaningfully to your overarching business mission.

Outline: Start by detailing your business's prime directives by deconstructing each expansive goal into actionable steps with measurable outcomes. Execute by defining key initiatives, allocating resources and setting timelines to ensure accountability and accelerate progress.

CONSTRUCT MY CORE TIMESLINES

What Deadlines Have You Set For Each Company Goal?

Right Now: You are identifying and establishing a concrete timeline for achieving your goals and objectives.

KEY TAKEAWAY

Recognize that: Your Core Timelines instill urgency, sustain momentum and enforce operational focus. Constructing this structured schedule with clear milestones and deadlines translates strategy into actionable steps, prevents drift, and energizes execution across your enterprise.

KEY ACTION

Outline: Start by detailing your pivotal milestones and the action steps needed to meet target completion due dates. Execute by creating a game plan that prioritizes tasks, allocates resources and maintains momentum - ensuring progress toward tangible results.

KEY NOTES

CONSTRUT MY CORE METRICS

How Will You Measure Your Success?

Right Now: You are identifying and establishing the criteria, benchmarks and metrics to assess progress and success.

Recognize that your Core Metrics transform ambition into actionable insight by measuring what matters most. Constructing clear metrics and KPIs enables you to track performance, make data-driven decisions, and enhance transparency, ensuring alignment with your mission and goals.

Outline: Start by detailing your key performance indicators (KPIs) by identifying the most critical metrics to track business progress. Execute by aligning each KPI with strategic objectives, setting clear benchmarks and reviewing consistently to assess results and optimize execution.

DRAFTING YOUR STRATEGY STATEMENT

How Will I Actualize My Dream?

A crystallized strategy aligns your team, partners and stakeholders around a unified vision, driving focused efforts and coordinated execution. A well-defined Strategy Statement provides directional clarity, informs critical decisions and links daily operational work to long-term objectives.

Outline a focused and actionable set of core strategies by answering these four guiding questions:

What are your company's core goals?
Define the Big-Picture outcomes that your business is aiming to achieve - both visionary and practical.

What specific objectives will drive progress?
Identify short- to mid-term priorities that break your goals into measurable steps or initiatives.

What timelines will keep your momentum on track?
Set realistic yet ambitious timeframes to ensure accountability and focus across all stages of execution.

What key metrics will you track to measure success?
Select meaningful Key Performance Indicators (KPIs) that reflect real progress and guide decision-making.

DRAFTING MY STRATEGY STATEMENT

Capture the quintessence of your strategy—define decisive actions, key objectives and success metrics - to transform vision into execution and ambition into measurable gains.

Use the space below to write your strategy statement, crafting actionable goals, bolded priorities/opportunities, pivotal insights and the breakthrough realizations that sharpen your execution plan. Employ decisive next steps to transform vision into action and aspiration into impact.

MY STRATEGY STATEMENT DRAFT:

This is your space to crystallize your vision into a focused, actionable strategy that aligns priorities, drives execution and delivers results.

STEP 2:
KNOW THY CUSTOMER

"The customer is the business."
~ Peter Drucker (Author & Management Guru)

This is more commandment than mere step, for the ultimate key to success is not in simply offering a product or service but in truly understanding, then consistently delivering, exactly what your marketplace truly desires.

Acquiring and retaining revenue-generating customers is the foundation of sustainable income and business viability - making the cultivation of customer intelligence essential to sharpen decisions, align strategies and achieve desired outcomes across all time horizons.

Mastering customer understanding through accurate research, genuine empathy and forward-thinking analysis transforms transactions into meaningful relationships. Accurate customer analytics fuel growth, create loyal advocates and build enduring competitive advantages.

Ultimately, decoding and knowing the true profile of your customers combines deep insight with decisive action - anticipating unmet needs and delivering irresistible solutions that turn buyers into lifelong brand advocates, driving sustainable growth.

Remember that:
True customer mastery is a dynamic discipline, demanding relentless market immersion, a fusion of data-driven insight and intuitive judgment, and organizational agility to translate understanding into scalable action.

When you optimize this symbiotic relationship between insight and creation, you unlock the ultimate business advantage: a regenerative system where customer satisfaction fuels expansion and each success deepens your market intelligence - creating unstoppable momentum in any economic climate.

Those who master this discipline do not just adapt - they define the market's future, setting the pace for competitors to follow.

Developing a customer-first mindset is non-negotiable.

ARE YOU READY TO VIEW THE WORLD THROUGH THE HEART, MIND AND EYES OF YOUR CUSTOMERS?

KNOW THY CUSTOMER

TRIPLE PLAY STRATEGY

Ⓐ

RESEARCHING YOUR MARKETPLACE
How Much Demand Is There For Your Products?

Analyze My Target Markets

Analyze My Market Niche

Analyze My Competitors

Analyze My Market Trends

Ⓑ

MARKETING YOUR COMPANY
How Will You Attract Loyal Customers?

Define My Unique Value Proposition

Define My Marketing Channels

Define My Brand Story

Define My Customer Journey

Ⓒ

SELLING YOUR GOODS
How Will You Turn Prospects Into Paying Customers?

Set Up My Manufacturing

Set Up My Quality Control

Set Up My Customer Service

Set Up My Inventory

ARE YOU READY TO VIEW THE WORLD THROUGH THE HEART, MIND AND EYES OF YOUR CUSTOMERS?

RESEARCHING YOUR MARKETPLACE
How Much Demand Is There For Your Products?

🔒 KEY TACTICS

Analyze My Target Markets

What Are the Defining Dynamics of Your Marketplace?

Identify key traits and behaviors in your target market, including demographics, lifestyle and purchasing power.

Analyze My Market Niche

Who Exactly Are Your Target Customers?

Identify the marketing channels that align best with your target audience's preferences and behaviors.

Analyze My Competitors

Who Else Offers Similar Solutions?

Identify the strengths and weaknesses of both direct and indirect competitors to uncover market gaps.

Analyze My Marlet Trends

What Emerging Trends Are Impacting Your Industry?

Identify current and emerging trends in technology, consumer behavior, market dynamics and regulations.

By ***Researching Your Marketplace***, you become the cartographer of opportunity - mapping uncharted demand, decoding competitive landscapes, and discovering the precise intersections where customer needs meet your unique value proposition.

ANALYZE MY TARGET MARKET

Who Are Your Most Valuable Key Audiences?

Right now: You are identifying the defining dynamics and behaviors in your target market, including demographics, lifestyle and purchasing power.

KEY TAKEAWAY

Recognize that: Your Target Market analytics serve to shape your offerings, facilitating alignment with customer behaviors and preferences. Thoughtfully analyzing these forces enables you to design products and services that resonate, fostering loyalty and driving sustained business success.

KEY ACTION

Outline: Start by detailing the key demographics, distinctive behaviors, and influential psychographic factors relevant to your ideal market segments. Execute by applying these insights to shape product design and marketing strategies that resonate with your target audience.

KEY NOTES

ANALYZE MY MARKET NICHE

Who Exactly Are Your Core Customers?

Right now: You are identifying the marketing channels that align best with your target audience's preferences and behaviors.

▼ KEY TAKEAWAY

Recognize that: Your Market Niche serves as the strategic foothold for dominating specialized customer segments. Analyzing their underserved needs, purchasing triggers and emotional drivers converts generic outreach into hyper-relevant messaging that commands unwavering brand loyalty.

🔓 KEY ACTION

Outline: Start by detailing the distinctive traits, collective affinities and purchasing patterns of your primary customers. Execute by applying these insights to develop targeted brand messaging that evokes emotion and influences purchasing decisions.

✎ KEY NOTES

ANALYZE MY COMPETITIVE LANDSCAPE

Which Market Rivals Offer Similar Solutions?

Right now: You are identifying the strengths and weaknesses of both direct and indirect competitors to uncover market gaps and monetizable opportunities.

🔷 KEY TAKEAWAY

Recognize that: Your Competitive Landscape serves to expose rival weaknesses and whitespace opportunities. Thoughtfully analyzing competitor strategies, customer frustrations and market gaps lets you differentiate decisively, command premium positioning and attract underserved buyers.

🔓 KEY ACTION

Outline: Start by detailing each competitor's strengths, weaknesses, market position and strategies. Execute by proactively applying this analysis to sharpen your value proposition and directly address unmet needs and emerging opportunities your competitors may overlook.

✏️ KEY NOTES

ANALYZE MY MARKET TRENDS

What Emerging Trends Are Impacting Your Industry?

Right now: You are identifying current and emerging trends in technology, consumer behavior, market dynamics and regulations to capture new opportunities.

KEY TAKEAWAY

Recognize that: Your Market Trends serve as the early-warning system for industry disruption and opportunity. Thoughtfully analyzing technological shifts, behavioral changes and regulatory developments position you ahead of competitors, turning market volatility into competitive advantage.

KEY ACTION

Outline: Start by detailing key industry trends, noting paradigm-shifting technology, evolving customer preferences and regulations. Execute by translating these insights into actionable strategies that anticipate demand fluctuations and position your business for sustained competitive advantage.

KEY NOTES

DRAFTING MY MARKET RESEARCH

How Much Demand Is There for My Products?

A powerful market research plan synthesizes your customers' needs, competitors' gaps and industry trends into a sharp, actionable blueprint for dominance. An effective Market Research Report exposes opportunities, mitigates risks and aligns your business with real demand, ensuring every decision is grounded in insight, not instinct.

Outline a rigorous and insightfully clear market research plan by answering these four guiding questions:

Who is your ideal customer archetype?
Identify their core demographics and psychographics which include behaviors, decision-making triggers and pain points.

Where are you deliberately choosing to dominate?
Define your distinct market niche: the overlap of your specific strengths and customers' unmet needs that competitors overlook.

Who are you up against?
Map your competitors' strengths and weaknesses to pinpoint exactly where your solution can outperform and better serve the customer..

What emerging shifts create your strategic advantage?
Track technological, cultural and regulatory changes that will amplify your differentiators or render existing solutions obsolete.

DRAFTING MY MARKET RESEARCH

Capture the quintessence of your market's truth—its unspoken needs and untapped opportunities. Pursue rigor, incisive analysis and revelatory insights as you decode the patterns only your research can reveal.

Use the space below to architect your market insights, drawing from customer behaviors, competitive gaps, industry trends and actionable data. Employ decisive conclusions, bolded opportunities and transformative revelations to crystallize your market's future reality.

MY MARKET RESEARCH PLAN DRAFT:

This is your space to analyze, synthesize and activate your market's most pivotal truths.

MARKETING YOUR COMPANY
How Will You Attract Loyal Customers?

🔒 KEY TACTICS

Define My Unique Value Proposition

What Makes Your Company Stand Out?

Identify the transformative benefits only your business offers that make competitors irrelevant.

Define My Marketing Channels

Where Will You Reach Your Target Customers?

Identify the marketing channels that align best with your target audience's preferences and behaviors.

Define My Brand Story

What Narrative Will Forge Authentic Audience Connections?

Identify and create a compelling brand narrative that reflects your company's mission, vision and values.

Define My Customer Journey

How Will You Guide Prospects from Discover to Loyalty?

Identify each stage of your ideal customer's path and align your marketing, messaging and experiential strategies accordingly.

By ***Marketing Your Company***, you engineer emotional alchemy - converting passive audiences into fervent evangelists who do not merely buy your products but embody your mission, amplifying your influence through every interaction with market-shaping conviction.

DEFINE MY UNIQUE VALUE PROPOSITION

What Makes Your Company Stand Out?

Right now: You are identifying the irresistable benefits your business delivers, those market-shaping differentiators that command attention.

Recognize that: Your Unique Value Proposition (UVP) serves as the foundation of compelling brand messaging, crystallizing your competitive edge in ways customers instantly understand. Defining your UVP allows you to articulate not just what you offer, but why customers should choose you.

Outline: Start by detailing the core benefits your goods deliver and by effectively highlighting your distinct advantages. Execute by conducting a thorough competitive analysis to emphasize how your innovation, quality or results consistently outperform alternatives.

DEFINE MY CHANNELS

Where Will You Reach Your Target Customers?

Right now: You are identifying the marketing channels that align best with your target audience's preferences and behaviors.

KEY TAKEAWAY

Recognize that: Your Marketing Channels serve to maximize engagement by connecting with audiences in their natural environments. Defining your marketing channels strategically ensures your visibility where customers actively spend time, amplifying both reach and conversion potential.

KEY ACTION

Outline: Start by detailing the most effective marketing platforms for your audience and design a multi-channel strategy that engages them at every touchpoint. Execute by leveraging data-driven insights to optimize your approach, maximizing reach, conversions and customer loyalty.

KEY NOTES

DEFINE MY BRAND STORY

What Narrative Will You Tell to Connect With Your Audience?

Right now: You are identifying and creating a compelling brand narrative that reflects your company's mission, vision and values.

Recognize that: Your Brand Story serves to build a memorable and distinctive identity, allowing customers to connect with your brand on both a personal and emotional level. Defining an authentic, captivating brand story humanizes your brand and deeply aligns with audience values.

Outline: Start by detailing your company's origin, mission and key milestones - focusing on how your business positively impacts customers' lives. Execute by crafting a resonant story that illustrates how your solutions enhance daily experiences and foster emotional connection.

DEFINE MY CUSTOMER JOURNEY

How Will You Guide Prospects from Discover to Loyalty?

Right now: You are identifying each stage of your ideal customer's path and align your marketing, messaging and experience strategies accordingly.

KEY TAKEAWAY

Recognize that: Your Customer Journey is essential for guiding individuals from first impression to brand advocacy. Defining each stage: awareness, consideration, purchase, retention and advocacy - enables you to align your customer experience strategies to effectively meet thier needs.

KEY ACTION

Outline: Start by detailing all the touchpoints and interactions your ideal customer encounters at each stage of their buying process. Execute by leveraging this holistic understanding to deliver consistent, personalized experiences that nurture brand loyalty and drive sustainable growth.

KEY NOTES

DRAFTING MY MARKETING CAMPAIGN

How Will We Attract Loyal Customers?

A powerful campaign synthesizes your value proposition, audience psychology and competitive differentiators into a unified strategic weapon. An effective Campaign Blueprint exposes conversion pathways, maximizes message resonance and outmaneuvers market noise - ensuring your marketing operates as a precision-guided system.

Outline an irresistible and high-converting marketing campaign by answering these four guiding questions:

What's your irresistible promise?
Distill your unfair advantage into one benefit-driven statement that makes competitors irrelevant.

Where does your audience engage?
Identify and dominate the high-impact platforms where your customers actively seek solutions, not just content.

How will you forge emotional bonds?
Weave authentic narratives that make customers see themselves in your mission, not just your product.

What's the conversion path from curiosity to loyalty?
Engineer a seamless progression from discovery to repeat purchase - with strategic value reinforcement at each stage.

DRAFTING MY MARKETING CAMPAIGN

Capture the quintessence of your campaign's potential—its most persuasive narratives and top-converting pathways. Pursue bold creativity, data-driven experimentation and emotional resonance as you craft the engagement only your brand can deliver.

Use the space below to architect your campaign blueprint, drawing from audience psychology and conversion drivers. Employ tested hypotheses and journey mapping to realize your campaign's maximum impact.

MY MARKETING CAMPAIGN DRAFT:

This is your space to architect, pressure-test and optimize your campaign's most powerful conversion levers.

©

SELLING YOUR GOODS
How Will You Turn Prospects Into Paying Customers?

KEY TACTICS

Set Up My Manufacturing Process

How Will You Produce Your Company's Products?

Identify the critical details of your production and delivery cycles from initiation to final fulfillment.

Set Up My Quality Assurance

How Will You Meet Your Customer Requirements?

Identify the specific methods your company will use to enforce consumer quality standards are met.

Set Up My Customer Support

How Will You Keep Your Customers Happy?

Identify every key process you have in place to consistently and effectively exceed customer expectations.

Set Up My Stock Control

How Will You Maintain Inventory to Meet Demand Efficiently?

Identify a structured inventory management process that ensures product availability without overstocking.

By ***Selling Your Goods***, you transform initial interest into decisive action - skillfully guiding customers from awareness to purchase while building lasting value and fostering relationships that encourage repeat business and long-term loyalty.

SET UP MY MANUFACTURING PROCESS

How Will You Produce Your Company's Products?

Right now: You are identifying the critical details of your production and delivery cycles from initiation to final fulfillment.

Recognize that: Your Manufacturing Process is the backbone of your product business, ensuring consistent quality, scalable output and cost efficiency. Setting up production methods that align with your brand promise reinforces your market position and builds customer trust.

Outline: Start by detailing your production workflow step-by-step - from sourcing to final assembly - including partners, equipment and quality checks. Execute by optimizing for speed, cost, service and/or uniqueness to outperform the marketplace.

SET UP MY QUALITY ASSURANCE

How Will You Meet Your Customer Requirements?

Right now: You are identifying the specific methods your company will use to ensure consumer quality standards are met.

KEY TAKEAWAY

Recognize that: Your Quality Assurance fosters trust and loyalty by delivering flawless products that consistently surpass expectations, effectively minimizing risks. Align QA processes with industry benchmarks and evolving customer needs to ensure unmatched quality.

KEY ACTION

Outline: Start by detailing your end-to-end quality control program - from initial inspections to final product testing including accountability measures. Execute by leveraging technology and training to ensure excellence and continuous improvement throughout your production.

KEY NOTES

SET UP MY CUSTOMER SUPPORT

How Will You Keep Your Patrons Happy?

Right now: You are identifying every key process you have in place to consistently and effectively exceed customer expectations.

🔻 KEY TAKEAWAY

Recognize that: Your Customer Support transforms satisfied buyers into advocates, distinguishing your brand in competitive markets. Setting up your service model to meet customer expectations ensures a seamless experience that builds trust and long-term loyalty.

🔓 KEY ACTION

Outline: Start by detailing your omnichannel customer service strategy including response times, escalation paths, empowerment tools with key metrics to track satisfaction. Execute by equipping agents with AI-driven support, comprehensive training and community-building initiatives.

✏️ KEY NOTES

SET UP MY INVENTORY MANAGEMENT

How Will You Maintain Stock to Meet Demand Efficiently?

Right now: You are identifying a structured inventory management process that ensures product availability without overstocking.

Recognize that: Your Inventory Management serves as the heartbeat of your operations, balancing stock levels to prevent shortages or overages. Setting up your system to align with demand patterns ensures efficient operations and meets customer expectations.

Outline: Start by detailing your end-to-end protocol from forecasting to reorder triggers and stock audits, while identifying key metrics (turnover ratio, fill rate) to track efficiency. Execute by leveraging automation, demand planning tools or vendor partnerships to stay lean yet responsive.

DRAFTING MY SALES STRATEGY

How Will We Turn Prospects Into Paying Customers?

A powerful sales strategy sseamlessly integrates your ideal customer profile, compelling value proposition and optimized conversion pathways into a revenue engine. An effective Sales System uncovers key buying triggers and maximizes customer lifetime value - transforming transactions into enduring, loyal relationships.

Outline a relentless and revenue-driving sales strategy by answering these four guiding questions:

How will you deliver on your promise?
Detail production models, quality benchmarks and contingency plans.

How will you maintain product excellence?
Implement thorough checking systems and defect resolution at every stage, with procedures to fix issues before products ship.

How will you build lasting customer relationships?
Create reliable support channels with trained staff, response standards and loyalty drivers that keep customers coming back.

How will you ensure product availability?
Develop smart inventory systems that track stock levels in real time and prevent shortages or overstocking.

DRAFTING MY SALES STRATEGY

Capture the quintessence of your sales advantage - its most persuasive differentiators and frictionless conversion pathways. Pursue relentless execution and client-centric innovation as you build your business.

Use the space below to architect your sales mastery, drawing from ideal buyer psychology, competitive gaps, process efficiencies and growth levers. Employ battle-tested tactics, bolded win-rate boosters and pipeline accelerators to manifest your sales dominance.

MY SALES STRATEGY DRAFT:

This is your space to design, pressure-test and optimize the revenue conversion systems that transform prospects into profit.

STEP 3:
GET IT ORGANIZED

"For every minute spent in organizing, an hour is earned."
~ Benjamin Franklin (Founding Father & Inventor)

Once you have chosen your company's goods and services, it is critical to build solid operational systems and organizational structure to support them.

Organizational Planning never stops evolving – it is the deliberate practice of scrutinizing what works, reshaping what doesn't and reimagining what is next to future-proof your business.

You can think of the organizational plan as basically the "TO-DO" List for your company. Be proactive to ensure that all risk factors, legalities and local regulations are considered and dealt with properly at the right times.

Today's exceptional companies execute with precision, yet remain agile, embedding continuous improvement into their culture and empower their teams to make decisions within clear strategic boundaries.

Ultimately, a systematized enterprise thrives amid uncertainty - where strategic infrastructure becomes your leverage point, optimizing resources, anticipating challenges and converting market opportunities into measurable advantage.

Remember that:
Business organization is not a destination but a continuous refinement and strategic thinking journey. It requires discipline, foresight and an unwavering commitment to excellence - because the structures you build today determine the agility and scale you will command tomorrow.

As an entrepreneur, your ability to create and maintain an responsive and adaptive organizational framework will be critical to your venture's long-term success.

Embrace this process not as a bureaucratic or administrative necessity but as a strategic advantage that will distinguish your business in an increasingly complex and competitive marketplace.

The most enduring companies are not just well-run; they are deliberately architected to learn, pivot and lead.

ARE YOU WILLING TO TAKE THE LEGAL STEPS NECESSARY TO MAKE YOUR BUSINESS OFFICIAL?

GET IT ORGANIZED

TRIPLE PLAY STRATEGY

Ⓐ

ESTABLISHING YOUR BRAND
What Image Will Your Company Present?

Select My Brand Name
Select My Brand Logo
Select My Brand Tagline
Select My Brand Voice

Ⓑ

CAPITALIZING YOUR VENTURE
How Will Your Company Be Financed?

Determine My Startup Resources
Determine My Startup Costs
Determine My Startup Budgets
Determine My Startup Funding

Ⓒ

FORMING YOUR ORGANIZATION
What Legal Form Is Best For Your Company?

Structure My Entity
Structure My Licenses
Structure My Insurance
Structure My Taxes

ARE YOU WILLING TO TAKE THE LEGAL STEPS NECESSARY TO MAKE YOUR BUSINESS OFFICIAL?

ESTABLISHING YOUR BUSINESS BRAND
What Image Will Your Company Present to the World?

Select My Brand Name

What Will Your Company and Its Products Be Called?

Identify product names that personify your brand identity and uniquely represent your business vision.

Select My Brand Logo

What Images, Colors or Words Best Symbolize Your Company?

Identify distinctive graphic designs, shapes or textual graphics that best represent your business's identity and values.

Select My Brand Tagline

What Phrase Effectively Captures Your Brand's Essence?

Identify a slogan, statement or set of words that powerfully conveys your company's vision, values and purpose.

Select My Brand Voice

How Will Your Company Express Its Identity?

Identify the tone, style and language that authentically reflect your brand's unique personality and values.

By ***Establishing Your Business Identity***, you cultivate a distinctive and memorable presence that strategically communicates your enterprise's core value proposition, authentic differentiators and guiding principles thus resonating deeply with your ideal audience and positioning you ahead of competitors.

SELECT MY NAME

What Will Your Company and Its Products Be Called?

Right now: You are identifying the product names that personify your brand identity and uniquely represent your business vision.

KEY TAKEAWAY

Recognize that: Your Brand Name serves as the cornerstone of customer perception and market positioning. Selecting a name that balances memorability, audience resonance and brand values accelerates recognition, fosters emotional connections and creates a foundation for marketing efforts.

KEY ACTION

Outline: Start by detailing prime keywords related to your industry, mission or unique selling point, then experiment with combinations or creative twists. Execute creative brainstorming to generate 3-5 name candidates, then vet each for trademarks, market resonance and alignment with your brand identity.

KEY NOTES

SELECT MY LOGO

What Colors, Images or Words Best Symbolize Your Company?

Right now: You are identifying distinctive designs, symbols, shapes or textual graphics that best represent your business's identity and values.

Recognize that: Your Brand Logo and Color Palette serve as the emotional DNA encoding how customers feel about your brand. Selecting a consistent color scheme that reflects your brand's personality and elicits the desired emotions ensures strong appeal and recognition.

Outline: Start by detailing 3-5 logo concepts with color palettes that embody your brand's personality - balancing clarity, emotional resonance, and industry relevance. Execute competitive benchmarking and trend analysis to refine designs, ensuring visual distinction and instant recognition.

SELECT MY TAGLINE

What Slogan Best Clarifies Your Unique Selling Points?

Right now: You are identifying a slogan, statement or set of words that powerfully conveys your company's vision, values and purpose.

🔻 KEY TAKEAWAY

Recognize that: Your Brand Tagline encapsulates why customers should care, transforming vision, mission and values into visceral appeal. Selecting a tagline that conveys your brand's essence and offers compelling reasons for customer trust ensures your brand stands apart.

🔓 KEY ACTION

Outline: Start by detailing 3-5 potential taglines that distill your brand's essence—testing each for clarity, memorability, and competitive differentiation. Execute refinements by brainstorming key benefits, emotions or differentiators you want to highlight, then turn your ideas into short, catchy phrases.

✎ KEY NOTES

SELECT MY VOICE

How Will Your Company Communicate With Its Audience?

Right now: You are identifying the tone, style and language that authentically reflect your brand's unique personality and values.

Recognize that: Your Brand Voice builds trust and establishes an authentic connection with your audience, making your brand relatable and memorable across all touchpoints. Selecting your brand voice - whether formal, casual, humorous or authoritative - ensures consistency and recognition.

Outline: Start by detailing 3-5 distinct brand voice personas and draft messaging for each, gathering feedback to identify the style that best conveys your values. Execute targeted audience testing to identify which style best aligns with your values while maximizing emotional connection and recall.

DRAFTING MY BRANDING PLAN
What Image Will My Company Present to the World?

A powerful business identity consolidates your mission, operational ethos and market position into a competitive signature. An effective Business Identity galvanizes stakeholder trust, fuels operational excellence and propels market differentiation, ensuring your enterprise commands authority amid industry shifts.

Outline a distinctive and commanding business identity by answering these four guiding questions:

Is your name a strategic asset?
Choose a name and audit for instant recognition, memorability, relevance and scalability.

What emotions do your visuals evoke?
Choose simple, distinctive design elements that visually convey your company's personality and values.

Can you capture your essence in under 5 words?
Create a short, benefit-driven phrase that tells customers exactly why they should choose you.

How does your personality sound?
Codify your verbal fingerprint - whether professional, friendly or bold - that matches your brand personality.

DRAFTING MY BRANDING PLAN

Capture the quintessence of your business by articulating its core purpose, strategic value, and foundational strengths. Establish a clear identity through well-designed processes, scalable frameworks and robust governance standards.

Use this space to architect your business identity with core processes, scalability frameworks and governance standards. Employ replicable systems and continuous improvement to ensure measurable impact.

MY BUSINESS BRANDING DRAFT:

This is your space to codify, systematize and operationalize your business's structural advantage.

CAPITALIZING YOUR BUSINESS VENTURE
How Will Your Company Be Financed?

🔒 KEY TACTICS

Determine My Startup Investment

What Will It Take to Launch Successfully?

Identify how much seed money you'll need to cover fixed costs, variable expenses and contingencies to launch with confidence.

Determine My Startup Resources

What Will I Need to Operate Day-by-Day?

Identify the essential tools, talent and technology needed to run your business efficiently and ensure smooth operations.

Determine My Startup Budgets

How Will I Allocate Funds?

Identify how to allocate startup capital strategically, balancing essential expenditures with growth-focused investments.

Determine My Startup Funding

How Will I Finance My Business Launch?

Identify the funding mix that aligns with your business model, growth objectives and risk tolerance for a sustainable launch.

By *Capitalizing Your Business Venture*, you secure strategic funding to fuel your launch, intelligently navigate early-stage growth and establish scalable revenue streams thus laying the financial foundation for long-term profitability and competitive resilience in your market.

DETERMINE MY STARTUP INVESTMENTS

How Much Seed Money Is Necessary To Open?

Right now: You are identifying how much captital you will need to cover fixed costs, variable expenses and contingencies to launch with confidence.

Recognize that: Your Startup Investments serve as the financial launchpad to profitability and scalability. Determining exact figures for equipment, licenses and operating reserves prevents undercapitalization while optimizing initial spend for sustainable growth.

Outline: Start by detailing all anticipated expenses, categorizing as "one-time" versus "recurring" costs to build a realistic foundation. Execute expert validation by pressure-testing figures with seasoned founders, exposing blind spots and boosting budget credibility.

DETERMINE MY STARTUP RESOURCES

What Are the New Venture Assets Needed to Start?

Right now: You are identifying the essential tools, talent and technology needed to run your business efficiently and ensure smooth operations.

KEY TAKEAWAY

Recognize that: Your Startup Resources - physical, intellectual or human - serve as the fuel propelling your vision from concept to market dominance. Determining the precise mix of talent, tools and capital creates competitive velocity while safeguarding against operational burnout.

KEY ACTION

Outline: Start by detailing a comprehensive list of every resource your startup requires, from physical tools and software to human capital and funding. Execute by sorting into "must-have now" and "can-add later," using free tools, borrowing or bartering to cut costs while testing your idea.

KEY NOTES

DETERMINE MY STARTUP BUDGET

How Will You Utilize Your Business Capital Funds?

Right now: You are identifying how to allocate startup capital strategically, balancing essential expenditures with growth-focused investments.

KEY TAKEAWAY

Recognize that: Your Startup Budget serves as your financial blueprint to confront reality, prioritize ruthlessly and maximize every dollar. Determining a proper budget is essential for effective financial management, helping you track profitability to achieve long-term success.

KEY ACTION

Outline: Start by detailing your projected monthly expenses (fixed and variable) and revenue across pessimistic, realistic, and optimistic scenarios. Execute by tracking actual numbers in a streamlined spreadsheet or accounting tool, adjusting quickly when necessary.

KEY NOTES

DETERMINE MY STARTUP FUNDING

How Will I Finance My Business Launch?

Right now: You are identifying the funding mix that aligns with your business model, growth objectives and risk tolerance for a sustainable launch.

KEY TAKEAWAY

Recognize that: Your Startup Funding Strategy serves to lay the groundwork for your launch and long-term sustainability. Determining the right funding option means understanding the implications for control, repayment obligations and growth.

KEY ACTION

Outline: Start by detailing a list of viable funding sources, then assess each for accessibility, reliability and alignment with your financial goals. Execute by calculating costs (interest, equity dilution) and risks to ensure they fit your startup's financial strategy.

KEY NOTES

DRAFTING MY CAPITALIZATION PLAN
How Will My Company Be Financed?

Capitalization is not just funding, it is your strategic accelerator for scaling. A formidable Capitalization Plan secures vital resources, harnesses strategic financial power, and preserves steadfast control while igniting exponential growth. This exercise transforms projections into a launch-pad for triumph.

Outline a strategic and empowering capitalization plan by answering these four guiding questions:

What's the true cost of launch?
Break down one-time vs. recurring costs - make sure to include obvious costs (tools, permits) and hidden ones (training, backup funds).

What capital can you deploy immediately?
Take stock of all your resources: personal cash savings, assets you can sell, and the value of unpaid work you're putting in - sweat equity.

Where will each dollar create impact?
Focus spending on what directly acquires customers or delivers your product - delay or eliminate everything else.

What's your optimal capital strategy?
Determine whether it will be slow-but-steady self-funding or accelerated investor-backed growth best serves your vision.

DRAFTING MY CAPITALIZATION PLAN

Capture the quintessence of your financial architecture - its most strategic leverage points and growth accelerators. Pursue disciplined valuation and optimal funding structures as you crystallize your capitalization plan.

Use the space below to architect your funding mastery, drawing from runway targets, dilution thresholds, alternative financing and exit horizons. Employ ironclad projections, bolded liquidity events and scenario modeling to manifest your financial sovereignty.

MY CAPITALIZATION PLAN DRAFT:

This is your space to clarify, structure and operationalize your business's funding strategy.

FORMING YOUR BUSINESS ORGANIZATION
What Legal Form Is Best For Your Company?

Structure My Business Entity

What Form of Ownership Is Best For Your Company?

Identify the most suitable corporate structure (sole proprietorship, partnership, corporation) based on liability, taxes and growth.

Structure My Business Licenses

What Laws Do You Need to Comply With?

Identify local rules, permits and regulations required to operate legally, ensuring compliance and minimizing legal risks.

Structure My Business Insurance

How Are You Mitigating Business Risks?

Identify insurance options that safeguard your business and personal assets, covering liability, property and compensation.

Structure My Business Taxes

What Tax Obligations Must Your Business Meet?

Identify your business's federal, state, and local tax obligations, including income, sales, payroll and other taxes.

By ***Forming Your Business Organization***, you architect the structural foundation for decisive, future-proof governance thus enabling data-driven decisions that fuel operational resilience, accelerate disciplined scaling and compound competitive advantage for enduring market leadership.

STRUCTURE MY ENTITY

What Form of Ownership Is Best For Your Company?

Right now: You are identifying the most suitable corporate structure based on legal liabilities, taxes and future expansion needs.

💎 KEY TAKEAWAY

Recognize that: Your Legal Business Entity legal structure of your business will have long-term implications on your taxes, liability and overall management responsibilities. Structuring your organization is not just about compliance, but also about aligning with your goals, resources and risk tolerance.

🔓 KEY ACTION

Outline: Start by detailing the main business entity options (Sole Proprietorship, LLC, Corporation, Partnership), including their legal obligations, tax implications and operational complexity. Execute by assessing how each structure impacts funding potential to choose the optimal fit.

✏️ KEY NOTES

STRUCTURE MY LICENSES
What Laws Do You Need To Comply With?

Right now: You are identifying the rules, permits and regulations required to operate legally, ensuring compliance and minimizing legal risks.

Recognize that: Your Business Licenses, proper permits and adherence to all compliance requirements establish legal operation, shielding your enterprise from costly setbacks. Structuring these obligations with diligence safeguards your business against potential penalties and legal challenges.

Outline: Start by detailing licensing and permit requirements across three levels: federal (industry-specific regulations), state (business entity registration) and local (zoning laws, ordinances). Execute by assessing each structure's funding impact to choose the optimal framework.

STRUCTURE MY INSURANCE

How Are You Mitigating Operational Risks?

Right now: You are identifying insurance policies and coverage options that safeguard your business and personal assets, covering liability, property and compensation.

KEY TAKEAWAY

Recognize that: Your Business Insurance serves to provide protection against industry-specific risks, protecting against potential liabilities. Structuring your coverage properly ensures you can pursue growth opportunities confidently, without jeopardizing your assets or livelihood.

KEY ACTION

Outline: Start by detailing on three core policies: liability (lawsuit protection), property (physical assets) and industry-specific (e.g., malpractice or cyber risks). Execute by thoroughly reviewing policy terms, exclusions and coverage limits to identify and address any protection gaps.

KEY NOTES

STRUCTURE MY TAXES

What Tax Obligations Must Your Business Meet?

Right now: You are identifying your business's federal, state and local tax obligations, including income, sales, payroll and other taxes.

Recognize that: Your Business Taxes and adhering to filing deadlines are essential for consistent tax management and timely compliance. Structuring your tax obligations properly and with prudence enhances long-term financial stability and reinforces credibility with stakeholders.

Outline: Start by detailing on three core obligations: earnings reporting, tax liabilities and deductible expenses. Execute by implementing systems for each applicable tax type - preserving capital and preventing costly surprises through disciplined management.

DRAFTING MY ORGANIZATIONAL PLAN
What Legal Form Is Best For My Company?

Your business is not just an idea, it' i a precision-engineered legal and operational machine. This is the blueprint for turning vision into a self-sustaining, future-proof enterprise from Day One. This exercise transforms structure into competitive advantage, ensuring seamless execution and institutional resilience at scale.

Outline an unshakable and scalable organizational plan by answering these four guiding questions:

What structure shields your dreams and protects your venture?
Choose based on liability, taxes and growth: Sole Prop/LLC (Simple, but limited protection) vs. S/C-Corp (Investor-ready, complex compliance).

What safeguards protect your assets?
Identify essential coverage: General liability, E&O, cyber, property, workers' compensation, etc.

What permits and policies are non-negotiable?
Map compliance requirements: Licenses, industry-specific certifications and local regulations.

How will you stay audit-proof?
Keep clean records, systemize your accounting, pay estimated taxes quarterly and work with professional advisors.

DRAFTING MY ORGANIZATIONAL PLAN

Capture the quintessence of your operational backbone – its structural integrity and scaling mechanisms. Pursue airtight governance, process mastery, and resilience as you crystallize your organizational framework.

Use the space below to architect your operating system, drawing from compliance architectures, team workflows, risk redundancies, and control points. Employ battle-tested protocols, bolded efficiency levers and future-proof systems to manifest your operational dominance.

MY ORGANIZATIONAL PLAN DRAFT:

This is your space to define, establish and operationalize your business's legal and organizational foundation.

STEP 4:
CRAFT YOUR BUSINESS PLAN

"If you don't know where you're going, any road will get you there."
~ Lewis Carroll (Author Alice in Wonderland)

Every new startup company can benefit tremendously from the preparation of a well-thought-out and organized business plan.

Prudent business planning creates both a roadmap for success and a navigational system to keep your entrepreneurial journey aligned with its highest potential.

Embarking on startup business planning transcends mere administrative exercise — it's a strategic crucible that forges clarity from ambiguity. This disciplined process compels founders to distill their vision into actionable intelligence and establish measurable objectives that align ambition with execution.

Regularly revisiting and refining your plan allows you to adjust your strategies in real-time, ensuring you remain agile and responsive to any changes in the business environment.

Ultimately, a business plan is far more than a document - it is a strategic compass - a lens of strategic discernment that illuminates every critical decision and optimizes resource allocation for maximum impact.

Remember that:
Your business plan is the foundation upon which your startup is built — a powerful strategic tool that brings clarity, accountability and adaptability to your entrepreneurial endeavors.

It transforms abstract ideas into actionable strategies, creating a roadmap that not only directs your path but also inspires confidence in potential investors, partners and team members.

A business plan is not a static relic but a living, breathing framework — a dynamic compass that evolves in lockstep with your venture.

With stready diligence your plan adapts to market currents, scales with organizational complexity and matures alongside your leadership.

This blueprint turns vision into a roadmap for measurable success.

**ARE YOU READY TO PUT IT ALL INTO WORDS
AND COMMIT YOUR PLANS TO PAPER?**

CRAFT YOUR BUSINESS PLAN

TRIPLE PLAY STRATEGY

Ⓐ

DEVELOPING YOUR MARKETING STRATEGY
How Will You Acquire Loyal Customers?

Articulate My Business Concept

Articulate My Product Lines

Articulate My Sales Promotions

Articulate My Target Audiences

Ⓑ

ESTABLISHING YOUR OPERATIONAL FRAMEWORK
How Will You Achieve Your Business Vision?

Examine My Manuffacturing Process

Examine My Business Location

Examine My Company Inventory

Examine My Supply Chain

Ⓒ

MAPPING OUT YOUR FINANCIAL ROADMAP
How Will You Measure Your Profitability?

Calculate My Cash Flow

Calculate My Break-Even Point

Calculate My Balance Sheet

Calculate My Financial Projections

ARE YOU READY TO PUT IT ALL INTO WORDS AND COMMIT YOUR PLANS TO PAPER?

DEVELOPING YOUR MARKETING STRATEGY
How Will You Acquire Loygal Customers?

Articulate My Business Concept

What Is the Big Idea Behind Your Business?

Identify exactly what your business will do, why you do it and the unique value it provides to your target demographics.

Articulate My Product Lines

What Exactly Is Your Company Selling?

Identify the unique features, benefits, and competitive advantages of the products or services your company offers.

Articulate My Sales Promotions

How Will You Spark Interest and Drive Sales?

Identify the promotional strategies you'll use to create urgency, boost visibility and encourage customer action.

Articulate My Target Audiences

Who Exactly Is Your Ideal Customer?

Identify the specific demographics, behaviors, and preferences of your target market.

By ***Developing Your Marketing Strategy*** with precision and foresight, you craft a dynamic, data-driven roadmap that not only engages target audiences with pinpoint accuracy but also outmaneuvers competitors, optimizes conversion pathways and drives growth that transcends conventional planning limitations.

ARTICULATE MY BUSINESS CONCEPT
What Is the Big Idea Behind Your Business?

Right now: You are identifying specifically what your business will do, why you do it and the unique value it provides to your target demographics.

🔻 KEY TAKEAWAY

Recognize that: Your Business Concept serves as the nucleus that crystallizes your brand's purpose, audience and unique value. Articulating this foundation with precision ensures marketing cohesion, competitive differentiation and customer connections that convert interest into loyal advocacy.

🔓 KEY ACTION

Outline: Start by detailing 3-5 variants adressing different customer profiles of a one-sentence pitch: "We help [target audience] achieve [specific outcome] by [unique method]." Execute rapid validation by testing clarity with focus groups and refining until instantly understandable.

✏️ KEY NOTES

ARTICULATE MY PRODUCT LINES

What Exactly Is Your Company Selling?

Right now: You are identifying the unique features, benefits and competitive advantages of the products or services your company offers.

KEY TAKEAWAY

Recognize that: Your Product Lines serve as the tangible embodiment of your brand's problem-solving identity. Articulating their key features, benefits, and scalability demonstrates market relevance, strengthens customer trust and creates pathways for strategic expansion.

KEY ACTION

Outline: Start by detailing your core products or services in full detail, emphasizing their benefits, unique features and positioning. Execute strategic grouping to ensure alignment with your brand narrative and customer needs, while eliminating redundancies that dilute your marketing impact.

KEY NOTES

ARTICULATE MY SALES PROMOTIONS

How Will You Spark Interest and Drive Sales?

Right now: You are identifying the promotional activities that will capture your target audience's attention and motivate them to make a purchase.

KEY TAKEAWAY

Recognize that: Your Sales Promotions serve as the tactical sparkplugs that convert hesitation into revenue while preserving brand equity. Articulating these time-sensitive campaigns with strategic intent accelerates cash flow, attracts high-value buyers, and transforms first-time purchasers into loyal advocates.

KEY ACTION

Outline: Start by detailing your promotional mix—discount structures, urgency triggers (limited-time offers), loyalty incentives, and event-based activations. Execute controlled trials and testing across channels to optimize conversion rates while maintaining brand integrity and profit margins.

KEY NOTES

ARTICULATE MY TARGET AUDIENCES

Who Exactly Are You Trying to Reach and Serve?

Right now: You are identifying the demographics, behaviorial traits and preferences of the customers most likely to benefit from your product or service.

🔻 KEY TAKEAWAY

Recognize that: Your Target Audience serves as the strategic compass that directs all product development and messaging. Articulating their core motivations, unspoken frustrations and decision-making triggers ensures your solution resonates with surgical precision, converting indifference into urgent demand.

🔓 KEY ACTION

Outline: Start by detailing your audience's demographics (age/income), psychographics (values/frustrations), and buying behaviors. Execute data validation through customer surveys, competitor review analysis and targeted ad tests to sharpen your messaging and eliminate guesswork.

✏️ KEY NOTES

DRAFTING MY MARKETING STRATEGY
How Will We Acquire Loyal Customers?

A powerful marketing strategy synthesizes your brand's value, audience insights, and competitive whitespace into a relentless conversion engine. An effective Marketing Strategy galvanizes demand, fuels customer obsession, and propels market dominance, ensuring your message cuts through noise and drives measurable growth.

Outline an irresistible and high-converting marketing strategy by answering these four guiding questions:

Why will customers choose you over every alternative?
Expain why does the market needs your solution now in one sentence.

What's your must-have offer?
Articulate your signature product or service - its essential features, pricing tiers and why it's irresistible to your ideal customer.

How will you create buying urgency?
Use limited-time deals to spark first purchases, then keep them coming back with rewards for loyal buyers.

Who can't imagine life without you?
Describe the demographics and psychographics of your target market.

DRAFTING MY MARKETING STRATEGY

Capture the quintessence of your market approach—its positioning, audience resonance, and activation pathways. Pursue relevance, clarity and experimentation as you crystallize your company's acquisition engine.

Use the space below to architect your marketing strategy blueprint, drawing from positioning statements and customer personas. Employ focused outreach plans, bolded competitive advantages, and adaptive learning loops to accelerate momentum and drive sustainable growth.

MY MARKETING STRATEGY DRAFT:

This is your space to define, refine and commit to a clear customer growth plan rooted in real data and strategic clarity.

ESTABLISH YOUR OPERATIONAL FRAMEWORK
How Will You Achieve Your Business Vision?

🔒 KEY TACTICS

Examine My Manufacturing Process

How Are Your Goods Being Produced?

Identify the production process for each of your company's products and services.

Examine My Business Location

How Does Your Physical Location Impact Your Operations?

Identify the best suitable places to establish your base of operations and conduct business.

Examine My Company Inventory

How Will You Track All of Your Business Assets?

Identify the systems you will have set in place to protect company products, resources and supplies.

Examine My Supply Chain

How Will You Deliver Your Products/Services?

Identify all the processes that support the sourcing of raw materials, product delivery and supplier/vendor relationships.

By ***Establishing Your Operational Framework***, you systematically transform abstract strategies into actionable, high-performance processes that clearly define roles, standardize responsibilities, optimize resource allocations and streamline daily functions for maximum efficiency and scalability.

EXAMINE MY MANUFACTURING PROCESS
How Are Your Goods Being Produced?

Right now: You are identifying the methods and steps involved in your production workflow used to create each of your products and services.

Recognize that: Your Manufacturing Process serves as the quality heartbeat of your operation, sustaining product standards and profit vitality. Examining each production link—from sourcing to assembly—exposes efficiency gains that elevate output, reduce waste, and build growth-ready systems.

Outline: Start by detailing every step of your production workflow - from sourcing materials to packaging to final product delivery - to pinpoint inefficiencies. Execute granular process audits to expose hidden deficiencies and elevate output quality without compromising operational reliability.

EXAMINE MY BUSINESS LOCATION

How Does Your Physical Presence Impact Your Operations?

Right now: You are identifying the best suitable places to establish your base of operations and conduct commerce.

🔻 KEY TAKEAWAY

Recognize that: Your Business Location serves as the strategic nerve center for customer accessibility, operational efficiency, and brand perception. Examining its geographic advantages, daytime population, parking access and neighboring businesses ensures maximum visibility and spontaneous purchases.

🔓 KEY ACTION

Outline: Start by detailing 3-5 make-or-break location criteria factors: customer accessibility, cost efficiency and supply chain logistics. Execute real-world validation through short-term leases to pressure-test demand before committing, ensuring your location amplifies growth rather than constrains it.

✏️ KEY NOTES

EXAMINE MY COMPANY INVENTORY

How Will You Manage and Track Your Business Assets?

Right now: You are identifying the systems you will have set in place to protect company products, resources and supplies.

🔻 KEY TAKEAWAY

Recognize that: Your Company Inventory serves as the profit engine that powers cash flow while balancing customer demand. Examining stock levels, turnover ratios and seasonal trends prevents costly overages, eliminates stockouts and transforms idle products into working capital for strategic investments.

🔓 KEY ACTION

Outline: Start by detailing inventory management such as stock levels, storage and reorder points to ensure product availability without overstocking. Execute demand-driven replenishment to align levels with real-time sales data, preventing lost revenue from shortages and profit erosion from excess inventory.

✏️ KEY NOTES

EXAMINE MY SUPPLY CHAIN

How Will You Deliver Your Products/Services?

Right now: You are identifying each stage of your supply chain, from the sourcing raw materials to product delivery.

◆ KEY TAKEAWAY

Recognize that: Your Supply Chain serves as the operational lifeline that connects production to customer satisfaction. Examining each link—suppliers, logistics, and inventory nodes - prevents disruptions, safeguards profit margins and ensures scalable delivery systems that build market trust.

🔓 KEY ACTION

Outline: Start by detailing your supplier ecosystem - evaluating each for risks (location stability, quality control, pricing consistency) and diversification needs. Execute quarterly partnership reviews to secure bulk discounts, improve lead times and co-develop innovations that give you a market edge.

✎ KEY NOTES

DRAFTING MY OPERATIONAL FRAMEWORK
How Will We Achieve My Business Vision?

A powerful operational framework crystallizes your delivery excellence, risk mitigation and scalability into a growth engine. An effective Operational Framework fuels continuous improvement and propels institutional resilience - ensuring your business has the **flexibility to manage disruptions and drive continuous improvement.**

Outline an unshakable and scalable operational framework by answering these four guiding questions:

How will you balance cost and quality in your production?
Choose between in-house and outsourced, with clear benchmarks for defect rates and production lead times.

Does your physical/digital footprint strategically support your operational needs and financial objectives?
Choose a location that optimizes legal, tax and logistical advantages.

How will you turn stock into profit?
Align your inventory strategy with demand patterns to optimize cash flow, storage efficiency and fulfillment speed.

How will you ensure uninterrupted operations?
Create a flexible supply chain with backup suppliers and reliable logistics to serve your customers.

DRAFTING MY OPERATIONAL FRAMEWORK

Capture the quintessence of your operational engine - its delivery systems, internal rhythms and execution infrastructure. Pursue precision, resilience and adaptability as you crystallize your company's processes.

Use the space below to architect your operational framework, drawing from core workflows, resource flows, and execution checkpoints. Employ streamlined process steps, bolded efficiency gains and durable systems to support consistent value delivery and long-term scalability.

MY OPERATIONAL FRAMEWORK DRAFT:

This is your space to document, refine and strengthen the systems that bring your business vision to life.

MAPPING OUT YOUR FINANCIAL ROADMAP
How Will You Measure Your Profitability?

Calculate My Cash Flow

How Much Cash Do You Generate?

Identify the projected sales forecasts for each of your company's products and services.

Calculate My Break-Even Point

When Will Your Company Begin To Show A Profit?

Identify how many units of your products and services need to be sold in order to cover total costs.

Calculate My Balance Sheet

What Is Your Company's Financial Standing?

Identify all of your company's assets, liabilities, and calculate your total net worth. point in time.

Calculate My Financial Projections

What Are Your Future Revenue and Expense Estimates?

Identify the anticipated revenue streams and expenses over the next few years to gauge the financial viability of your business.

By ***Mapping Out Your Financial Roadmap*** with strategic precision, you establish clear, quantifiable benchmarks that track your enterprise's fiscal trajectory, assess operational viability in real-time and proactively identify growth opportunities while mitigating financial risks.

CONSTRUCT MY CORE OBJECTIVES

How Will You Reach Your Company's Goals?

Right Now: You are identifying the practical, actionable objectives that break down broad goals into manageable steps.

🔻 KEY TAKEAWAY

Recognize that: Your Core Objectives translate your company's high-level goals into precise, executable actions that fuel progress and performance. Constructing these objectives with clarity and alignment ensures that every initiative contributes meaningfully to your overarching business mission.

🔓 KEY ACTION

Outline: Start by detailing your business's prime directives by deconstructing each expansive goal into actionable steps with measurable outcomes. Execute by defining key initiatives, allocating resources and setting timelines to ensure accountability and accelerate progress.

✏️ KEY NOTES

CALCULATE MY BREAK-EVEN POINT

When Will Your Company Begin To Show A Profit?

Right now: You are identifying how many units of your products and services need to be sold in order to cover total costs.

Recognize that: Your Break-Even Point is the key make-or-break milestone where survival transitions to sustainable growth. Calculating fixed costs, variable margins and unit economics reveals the exact sales volume required to achieve financial independence and redirect capital toward strategic expansion.

Outline: Start by detailing your break-even point: divide fixed costs (rent, salaries) by unit margin (price minus variable costs). Execute quarterly reassessments to adapt to cost fluctuations, pricing shifts or demand changes - keeping profitability targets achievable and data-driven.

CALCULATE MY BALANCE SHEET

What Is the Financial Health of Your Business?

Right now: You are identifying all of your company's assets, liabilities and calculate your total net worth at this point in time.

Recognize that: Your Balance Sheet is the definitive snapshot of your company's financial stability, liquidity and capital structure. Calculating asset-to-liability ratios, working capital trends and equity changes pinpoints debt risks, unlocks idle assets and directs strategic capital allocation for maximum impact.

Outline: Start by detailing your financial shock absorbers - liquid assets (cash, receivables) and looming obligations (payroll, loans). Execute monthly balance sheet reconciliations to align assets/liabilities with equity, ensuring strategic agility and proactive startup risk management.

CALCULATE MY FINANCIAL PROJECTIONS

What Are Your Future Revenue and Expense Estimates?

Right now: You are identifying the anticipated revenue streams and expenses over the next few years to gauge the financial viability of your business.

🔻 KEY TAKEAWAY

Recognize that: Your Financial Projections are not crystal-ball fantasies, they are your navigational blueprint for survival and scaling. Calculating revenue trajectories, expense ratios and cash flow forecasts prevents blind spots, attracts investors and creates accountability for achieving major milestones.

🔓 KEY ACTION

Outline: Start by detailing 12-month financial forecasts including revenue streams, operating costs and cash flow trajectories. Execute monthly revisions using actual performance data and market shifts to maintain predictive accuracy and guide agile resource allocation.

✎ KEY NOTES

DRAFTING MY FINANCIAL ROADMAP
How Will We Measure Our Profitability?

A powerful financial roadmap crystallizes your capital strategy, profitability levers, and growth funding into an unstoppable economic engine. An effective Financial Roadmap galvanizes fiscal discipline, fuels strategic investment, and propels valuation growth, ensuring your enterprise thrives amid market volatility and scaling demands.

Outline a precision-engineered and growth-ready financial roadmap by answering these four guiding questions:

How will money move through your business?
Project monthly inflows (sales, investments) and outflows (fixed/variable costs) with a 3 month rolling forecast for liquidity.

When does your business fund itself?
Calculate your breakeven point then streamline costs and pricing to get there in a safe but rapid manner.

What's your true financial health?
Outline your company's assets, liabilities, equity structure and tracking methods to monitor and grow your net worth over time.

Where are you headed financially?
Model realistic 12–36 month revenue and expense forecasts, including conservative, aggressive and realistic scenarios.

DRAFTING MY FINANCIAL ROADMAP

Capture the quintessence of your financial roadmap - its funding priorities, cash flow logic and long-range fiscal design. Pursue clarity, discipline and adaptability as you crystallize your company strategy.

Use the space below to architect your financial roadmap, drawing from revenue projections, cost structures and growth benchmarks. Employ actionable calculations, bolded profitability drivers and smart efficiencies to steer your business toward enduring financial viability.

MY FINANCIAL ROADMAP DRAFT:

This is your space to chart, refine and validate the financial path that powers your business growth.

PROMOTE YOUR BRAND

"If you don't know where you're going, any road will get you there."
~ Lewis Carroll (Author Alice in Wonderland)

Now that you have lovingly created your company's brand identity with intention and care, the next critical step is to amplify it strategically to resonate deeply with your ideal audience.

Effective branding helps your customers understand who you are, what you do and why they should choose YOU over your competitors.

A powerful brand transcends logos and taglines; it is the living embodiment of your mission, values and the distinct emotional experience you deliver. Building a memorable brand will express your Unique Selling Proposition with precision, magnetize your ideal customers and elevate your reputation into a legacy.

Your brand is not just what you sell, but the story you tell and the connections you create in the marketplace.

Ultimately, promoting your brand effectively means building a lasting relationship with your audience, one that transcends mere transactions and fosters community around your values.

Remember that:
Successful brand promotion is an ongoing dialogue with your customers, continuously evolving to reflect their needs, aspirations and changing market dynamics.

By remaining authentic, responsive, and committed to your core mission, you transform your brand from a business entity into a meaningful experience that resonates deeply with your target audience.

No matter how innovative your products and services may be, impactful branding will set your company apart.

Functional branding fosters trust and loyalty, encouraging customers to return and advocate for your brand.

In today's crowded marketplace, establishing a distinct brand presence - both offline and online - is crucial for long-term success.

HOW ARE YOU POSITIONING YOUR COMPANY AND ITS PRODUCTS IN THE MARKETPLACE?

PROMOTE YOUR BRAND

TRIPLE PLAY STRATEGY

Ⓐ

PRODUCING YOUR SALES MATERIALS
How Will You Market Your Products & Services?

Craft My Sales Aresenal

Craft My Press Kit

Craft My Web Presence

Craft My Case Studies

Ⓑ

COORDINATING YOUR MARKETING & SALES
How Will You Keep Your Customers Happy?

Manage My Publicity Program

Manage My Public Relations

Manage My Sales Promotions

Manage My Customer Engagement

Ⓒ

GROWING YOUR BUSINESS NETWORK
How Will You Increase Your Profit Potential?

Expand My Connections

Expand My Alliances

Expand My Market Share

Expand My Professional Presences

HOW ARE YOU POSITIONING YOUR COMPANY AND ITS PRODUCTS IN THE MARKETPLACE?

PRODUCING YOUR SALES ARSENAL
How Will You Market Your Products & Services?

KEY TACTICS

Create My Sales Collateral

What Emotions Does Your Marketing Elicit?

Identify ways to present your business in the best light throughout multiple media channels.

Create My Press Kit

Are You Sharing Your Business Success With The Media?

Identify ways to package and present branded promotional materials to members of the media.

Create My Digital Presence

What Is The Status Of Your Online Properties?

Identify ways to drive people to your company website, social media and web directory listings.

Create My Case Studies

How Are You Showcasing Client Experiences to Build Trust?

Identify ways to showcase customer testimonials that highlight the positive experiences of your clients.

By ***Producing Your Sales Arsenal*** with precision and purpose, you engage your niche market in targeted dialogue, crafting high-impact brand assets that strategically amplify demand, differentiate your offerings and cultivate enduring customer loyalty.

CREATE MY SALES ARSENAL

Which Tools Will Elevate Your Customer Engagements?

Right now: You are identifying ways to present your business in the best light throughout multiple media channels.

KEY TAKEAWAY

Recognize that: Your Strategic Sales Collateral serves as the navigational toolkit for prospect decision-making, simplifying complex choices at each journey stage. Creating purpose-built assets including case studies, demos and comparison guides to bridge knowledge gaps, build consumer trust and drive conversions.

KEY ACTION

Outline: Start by gathering a suite of tailored assets - such as product brochures, case studies, pitch decks and testimonials that address specific pain points and objections. Execute with brand-consistent materials featuring clear calls to action to drive the next steps to a purchase.

KEY NOTES

CREATE MY PRESS KIT

Are You Sharing Your Business Success With The Media?

Right now: You are identifyingways to package and present branded promotional materials to members of the media.

KEY TAKEAWAY

Recognize Your Press Kit is essential for capturing media attention and conveying your brand's story effectively. Creating a digital-first repository complete with downloadable assets, boilerplates and executive bios - empowers journalists to develop stories with speed and context day or night.

KEY ACTION

Outline: Start by producing a press kit featuring your company overview, founder bios, high-res images, press releases, brand assets and contact details. Execute an appealing, informative kit that showcases your brand to the media. Ensure it is easily accessible, giving journalists everything they need to cover your story.

KEY NOTES

CREATE MY WEB PRESENCE

What Is The Status Of Your Online Properties?

Right now: You are identifying methods to attract and engage your target audience across your website, social media and directory listings.

🔶 KEY TAKEAWAY

Recognize that: Your Web Presence serves as the 24/7 global storefront for your brand, blending authority with accessibility across all digital touchpoints. Creating a cohesive, user-centric ecosystem establishes instant trust and converts passive visitors into loyal advocates.

🔓 KEY ACTION

Outline: Start by producing an online strategy that includes a responsive website, active social media profiles and optimized content for search engines. Execute by mapping your digital touchpoints to create a cohesive customer journey, while implementing calls-to-action that transform visitors into loyal customers.

✏️ KEY NOTES

CREATE MY CASE STUDIES

How Are You Showcasing Client Experiences to Build Trust?

Right now: You are identifying ways to showcase customer testimonials that highlight the positive experiences of your clients.

Recognize that: Your Customer Testimonials serve as powerful social proof, enhancing credibility and influencing potential buyers' decisions by letting authentic experiences validate your brand promise. Creating a library of real-world case-studies that demonstrate the tangible value of your offerings.

Outline: Start by gathering and presenting satisfied clients whose authentic feedback and success stories demonstrate your unique value proposition. Execute a testimonial strategy across key touchpoints to build social proof, shorten decision cycles and convert prospects through peer validation.

DRAFTING MY SALES ARSENAL PLAN
How Will We Market My Products & Services?

A powerful sales arsenal crystallizes your competitive edge, customer insights and conversion psychology into a relentless revenue generating force. An effective Sales Arsenal galvanizes interest, fuels desire and propels action - ensuring your message outmaneuvers competitors and closes deals at scale.

Outline an irresistible and deal-closing sales arsenal by answering these four guiding questions:

How will your sales materials instantly communicate value and convert interest into action?
Create crisp, compelling collateral that highlights your unique differentiators.

How will you make journalists' jobs easier?
Prepare a media-ready package that blends professionalism with personality to simplify the media's work.

Does your website captivate visitors and guide them toward meaningful engagement?
Implement SEO, blogs, landing pages and digital campaigns to expand your reach and attract leads.

How will you turn satisfied customers into your most persuasive advocates?
Capture authentic success stories in multiple formats, then weave them into every customer touchpoint to build trust and urgency.

DRAFTING MY SALES ARSENAL PLAN

Capture the quintessence of your sales advantage - its persuasive narratives and conversion pathways. Pursue messaging clarity, psychological triggers and competitive differentiation as you crystallize your selling system.

Use the space below to architect your materials, drawing from customer pain points, social proof and closing mechanics. Employ battle-tested scripts, conversion accelerators and irresistible promotional assets to manifest your revenue dominance.

MY SALES ARSENAL PLAN DRAFT:

This is your space to conceptualize, refine and elevate the tools that convert interest into action.

COORDINATING YOUR MARKETING & SALES
How Will You Keep Your Customers Happy?

🔒 KEY TACTICS

Manage My Publicity Program

How Will You Publicize Your Business?

Identify key strategies and campaigns that will generate news and free media attention for your brand.

Manage My Public Relations

How Will You Strengthen Trust and Credibility With the Public?

Identify key strategies and campaigns that will create a favorable public image for your business.

Manage My Sales Promotions

What Does Your Company Do Better Than The Competition?

Identify key strategies and campaigns that will increase brand awareness and boost business sales.

Manage My Customer Engagement

How Will You Build Relationships with Your Customers?

Identify key strategies and campaigns that will foster ongoing engagement and loyalty among your customer base.

By ***Coordinating Your Marketing and Sales*** efforts, you transform your business vision into market reality - strategically amplifying brand visibility through integrated advertising, public relations (PR), social media and content marketing campaigns that convert awareness into measurable growth.

MANAGE MY PUBLICITY

How Will You Publicize Your Business?

Right now: You are identifying the media strategies, programs, events and campaigns that will generate news and free media attention for your brand.

Recognize that: Your Strategic Publicity Program serves as the visibility accelerator that transforms brand awareness into market leadership. Effectively managing media relations and storytelling crafts compelling narratives, shapes public perception and builds trust with your core audiences.

Outline: Start by detailing a comprehensive publicity plan that includes identifying key media outlets, publishing press releases and engaging media. Execute strategic campaigns to position your brand as newsworthy to generate attention, awareness and credibility without advertising costs.

MANAGE MY PUBLIC RELATIONS

How Will You Build Public Trust & Credibility?

Right now: You are identifying key strategies and campaigns that will create a favorable public image for your business.

◈ KEY TAKEAWAY

Recognize that: Your Strategic Public Relations serves as the trust-engineering framework that converts credibility into competitive advantage. Effectively managing initiatives nurtures authentic stakeholder relationships and transforms values into visible community impact.

🔓 KEY ACTION

Outline: Start by detailing the core brand narratives, target audiences and outreach initiatives - press releases, media interviews, industry events, community involvement or partnership opportunities you will pursue. Execute a clear framework to nurture strong relationships with media and the public.

✎ KEY NOTES

MANAGE MY PROMOTIONS

How Will You Drive Immediate Customer Action?

Right now: You are identifying promotional sales strategies and incentive-based offers that will motivate customers to engage, purchase or return to your business.

Recognize that: Your Strategic Sales Promotions transform hesitation into immediate action—driving revenue through expertly crafted limited-time offers, product bundles and loyalty rewards. These tactics accelerate conversions, optimize inventory turnover and strengthen brand affinity.

Outline: Start by detailing a strategic mix of audience-targeted promotions like limited-time discounts, bundles, and referral incentives. Execute a promotional calendar featuring loyalty programs and referral campaigns, with tracking methods to optimize based on performance metrics.

MANAGE MY CUSTOMER ENGAGEMENT

How Will You Build Lasting Relationships With Your Customers?

Right now: You are identifying key strategies and campaigns that will foster ongoing interactions and loyalty among your customer base.

🔻 KEY TAKEAWAY

Recognize that: Your Strategic Customer Engagement serves as the loyalty flywheel that transforms satisfied buyers into brand advocates. Effectively managing personalized experiences, proactive responsiveness and community activation drives repeat purchases and referral pipelines.

🔓 KEY ACTION

Outline: Start by detailing your engagement strategy across channels including email, social media, in-person, and customer support with tailored messaging for each. Execute a feedback-driven approach using personalization and real-time responsiveness to deepen audience connections and brand loyalty.

✎ KEY NOTES

DRAFTING MY SALES AND MARKETING PLAN
How Will We Keep Our Customers Happy?

A powerful sales arsenal crystallizes your competitive edge, customer insights, and conversion psychology into a relentless revenue-generating force. An effective Sales Arsenal galvanizes interest, fuels desire, and propels action, ensuring your message outmaneuvers competitors and closes deals at scale.

Outline a unified and revenue-driving marketing & sales plan by answering these four guiding questions:

Where will you earn (not buy) attention?
Pursue high-impact media placements, influencer collaborations and attend industry events for earned credibility.

What core narratives or company messages do you want the public to know?
Craft clear messaging pillars and crisis protocols, ensuring every public interaction reinforces trust and aligns with your brand values.

What special offers, bundles or campaigns will you run to boost sales?
Launch limited-time campaigns that reward your best customers and attract high-value segments with clear KPIs to measure success.

How will you actively listen and respond to your customers across platforms?
Monitor customer sentiment using feedback loops to deepen loyalty and drive repeat purchases and referrals.

DRAFTING MY SALES & MARKETING PLAN

Capture the quintessence of your revenue engine—how your brand attracts, converts, and retains customers through your customer journey. Build a scalable system that unify your marketing and sales into one clear path.

Use the space below to architect your sales and marketing engine, drawing from data-driven lead thresholds and precision channel handoffs. Employ nurture flows, bolded triggers, and predictive alignment to conquer markets with velocity.

MY SALES A& MARKETING PLAN DRAFT:

This is your space to align, refine and strengthen the activities that drives awareness, conversion and long-term loyalty.

GROWING YOUR BUSINESS NETWORK
How Will You Increase Your Profit Potential?

Expand My Business Connections

Who Can Help Your Company Prosper?

Identify potential contacts and organizations you can collaborate on business projects together.

Expand My Business Alliances

What Organizations Can Help Your Company Improve?

Identify potential companies you can partner with to develop profitable business relationships.

Expand My Market Share

How Will Your Company Reach More of the Marketplace?

Identify potential new customer opportunities and distribution channels where you can sell your goods.

Expand My Professional Presence

How Will You Establish Yourself as an Industry Leader?

Identify key strategies and opportunities to enhance your visibility and reputation within your industry.

By ***Growing Your Business Network***, you systematically unlock high-value partnerships that accelerate brand authority, establish a strategic ecosystem for sustained goal achievement and deliver compounding returns on your relationship capital through trusted, mutually rewarding connections.

EXPAND MY CONNECTIONS
Who Can Accelerate Your Business Growth?

Identify key professionals, mentors and peers who offer insights, referrals and collaborations to expedite growth.

💎 KEY TAKEAWAY

Recognize that: Your Strategic Business Connections serve as the opportunity pipeline that fuels exponential growth and market intelligence. Expanding these relationships unlocks high-value partnerships, reveals untapped revenue streams and positions your venture as an industry collaborator of choice.

🔓 KEY ACTION

Outline: Start by detailing and listing high-value contacts and networking spaces including events, online platforms and industry groups to meet collaborators. Execute a strategy for authentic engagement through active listening, consistent follow-ups and equal value exchange to build lasting relationships.

✏️ KEY NOTES

EXPAND MY ALLIANCES

Who Can You Collaborate With to Accelerate Growth?

Identify partners, organizations, or leaders whose collaboration elevates your offerings, reach or credibility.

Recognize that: Your Strategic Business Alliances serve as the growth accelerators that multiply market reach and innovation capacity. Expanding these partnerships combines complementary strengths, unlocks co-created value and establishes competitive moats through shared strategic objectives.

Outline: Start by detailing strategic partnerships opportunities with suppliers, influencers, service providers or joint ventures - that align with your business goals. Execute partnership agreements offering mutual benefits that amplify your mission, visibility and customer value.

EXPAND MY MARKET SHARE

How Will Your Company Reach More of the Marketplace?

Identify untapped segments, audiences or regions where your offering meets demand and fuels growth.

▼ KEY TAKEAWAY

Recognize that: Your Market Share Growth serves as the resilience engine that compounds competitive advantage and industry influence. Expanding your share delivers scale efficiencies, cements category leadership and unlocks pricing power, future-proofing profitability amid market fluctuations.

🔓 KEY ACTION

Outline: Start by detailing strategies to grow your market share via product differentiation, targeting underserved segments and digital marketing expansion. Execute by researching viable new channels, platforms, demographics and regional markets that align with your capabilities and brand promise.

✎ KEY NOTES

EXPAND MY PROFESSIONAL PRESENCE

How Visible and Credible Are You in Your Industry?

Identify the platforms, networks and actions that will elevate your personal and professional profile.

Recognize that: Your Strategic Professional Presence serves as the credibility multiplier that opens doors to influence and opportunity. Expanding this visibility positions you as a thought leader, attracts high-value collaborations and elevates your organization's industry authority through visible expertise.

Outline: Start by detailing ways to elevate your industry presence through thought leadership, speaking engagements and strategic digital content. Execute a targeted content plan with articles, workshops and active social media engagement to build meaningful connections.

DRAFTING MY GROWTH & NETWORKING PLAN
How Will We Increase Our Profit Potential?

A powerful sales arsenal crystallizes your competitive edge, customer insights and conversion psychology into a relentless revenue generating force. An effective Sales Arsenal galvanizes interest, fuels desire and propels action, ensuring your message outmaneuvers competitors and closes deals at scale.

Outline a high-leverage and results-driven growth & networking plan by answering these four guiding questions:

Who are the key contacts, mentors or industry leaders that will accelerate your growth?
Cultivate a strategic network of pivotal relationships through consistent engagement - turning contacts into collaborators.

What potential partners, suppliers or collaborators align with your mission and offerings?
Forge win-win collaborations with complementary brands, formalizing alliances with clear roles and shared success metrics.

What underserved segments, geographic areas or industries can you target for growth?
Pinpoint market opportunities and leverage your competitive advantage to attract new customers.

How will you establish yourself as the expert in your space?
Define how you will showcase your brand and expertise across professional platforms and track the impact of these visibility efforts.

DRAFTING MY GROWTH & NETWORKING PLAN

Capture the quintessence of how your business will expand its reach and cultivate meaningful alliances. Pursue strategic clarity, bold outreach and high-impact relationship building as you shape your business network.

Use the space below to architect your company's key expansion tactics, strategic partnerships and scalable pathways. Leverage bold connections, untapped channels and relationship-driven strategies to accelerate growth and multiply impact.

MY GROWTH & NETWORKING PLAN DRAFT:

This is your space to map, refine and activate the connections and strategies that will scale your business reach and impact.

STEP 6:
CHIEF YOUR OPERATIONS

"Vision without execution is delusion."
~ Thomas Edison (Inventor & Businessman)

A successful business enterprise does not just appear magically with wishful thinking - you have to pay close attention to all the details.

Owning a viable operation hinges on how well you manage all of your business activities and how well you capitalize on opportunities in a timely fashion.

Operations are the lifeblood of enterprise - the vital force that animates strategy into sustainable success. Your leadership must ensure seamless synchronization between people, processes and technology, establishing clear KPIs that track progress toward mission-critical objectives.

Make innovation and flexibility fundamental to your company's DNA, creating systems that not only withstand change but harness it to propel growth.

Ultimately, operational excellence is not a destination but a relentless pursuit of mastery, where precision meets adaptability to forge enterprises that thrive amid volatility, transforming vision into enduring competitive advantage.

Remember that: Operational excellence separates market leaders from the rest.

Cultivate a culture of relentless refinement, insight-driven decisions and executional agility - where every process is a competitive advantage waiting to be optimized.

Embodying this disciplined approach builds an organizational engine capable of converting challenges into opportunities and aspirations into measurable impact.

True market leaders distinguish themselves through anticipatory agility - the ability to pivot before disruptions occur while consistently converting challenges into competitive advantages.

In today's volatile markets, adaptability is not just just survival; it's the blueprint for sustained dominance.

WHAT CAN MY COMPANY DO TO MAXIMIZE PROFITS AND MINIMIZE LOSSES?

CHIEF YOUR OPERATIONS

Ⓐ

GOVERNING YOUR VISION
Is Your Company Headed In the Right Direction?

Captain My Vision

Captain My Priorities

Captain My Activities

Captain My Performance

Ⓑ

MONITORING YOUR COMMUNICATIONS
Are You Getting Your Brand Message Across?

Describe My Manufacturing Process

Describe My Business Location

Describe My Company Inventory

Describe My Supply Chain

Ⓒ

CONTROLLING YOUR FINANCES
Are You Watching Your Budgets & Spending?

Supervise My Cash Flow

Supervise My Investments

Supervise My Net Worth

Supervise My Profit Margins

WHAT CAN MY COMPANY DO TO MAXIMIZE PROFITS AND MINIMIZE LOSSES?

GOVERNING YOUR VISION
Is Your Company Headed In the Right Direction?

Captain My Business Vision

Are You Supervising Your Goal Timelines?

Identify the current status of your objectives and review the milestones reached along the way.

Captain My Businses Priorities

What Will You and Your Company Accomplish Today?

Identify the marketing channels that align best with your target audience's preferences and behaviors.

Captain My Business Activities

Where Are You Investing Your Company's Resources?

Identify all current and ongoing projects within your company while maintaining a record of completed tasks.

Captain My Business Performance

How Well Is Your Business Performing Against Its Goals?

Identify key performance indicators that align with your business goals to effectively measure progress and inform strategic decisions.

By ***Governing Your Vision*** with clarity and purpose, you create the necessary structure, discipline and operational framework to seamlessly align daily business activities, team execution and resource allocation with long-term strategic objectives and sustainable success.

CAPTAIN MY VISION
Are You Supervising Your Goal Timelines?

Right now: You are identifying the current status of your objectives and review the milestones reached along the way.

🔻 KEY TAKEAWAY

Recognize that: Your Business Vision serves as the clear and compelling foundation for strategic decision-making and long-term success. Captaining this vision ensures organizational alignment, stakeholder inspiration and goal achievement, regardless of shifting market conditions.

🔓 KEY ACTION

Outline: Start by detailing your current strategic objectives, the milestones already achieved and any delays or adjustments needed. Execute progress reviews to address bottlenecks and recalibrate tactics - ensuring every effort compounds toward your long-term vision.

✏️ KEY NOTES

CAPTAIN MY PRIORITIES

What Will You and Your Company Accomplish Today?

Right now: You are identifying the most critical business priorities that support your strategic goals and require focused execution.

Recognize that: Your Business Priorities serve as the critical framework for resource alignment, decisive action and strategic execution. Captaining these priorities ensures operational agility, stakeholder confidence and impact delivery - regardless of evolving challenges.

Outline: Start by detailing your priorities by urgency and importance for the day, week or month. Execute focused daily reviews to ensure top-tier task completion, prune non-essential tasks, delegate responsiblities effectively and to channel all your resources toward your 3-5 highest-impact objectives.

CAPTAIN MY ACTIVITIES

Where Are You Investing Your Company's Resources?

Right now: You are identifying all current and ongoing projects within your company while maintaining a record of completed tasks.

◆ KEY TAKEAWAY

Recognize that: Your Business Activities serve as the vital engine driving operational excellence and profitability. Captaining these activities through strategic resource allocation and data-driven decisions ensures scalable growth and market resilience - regardless of inevitable economic shifts.

🔓 KEY ACTION

Outline: Start by detailing all mission-critical functions including operations, finance and growth that drive daily performance and strategic goals. Execute quarterly alignment audits to optimize systems, eliminate inefficiencies and pivot resources in response to market shifts or emerging opportunities.

✏️ KEY NOTES

CAPTAIN MY PERFORMANCE

How Well Is Your Business Performing Against Its Goals?

Right now: You are identifying key performance indicators that are essential for tracking your company's growth, productivity and success.

Recognize that: Your Business Performance serves as the definitive compass for operational success and profitability. Captaining these metrics through rigorous analysis and agile adjustments ensures financial health, strategic clarity and sustained achievement of critical goals.

Outline: Start by detailing the core metrics that define success for your business such as sales, customer satisfaction, productivity and financial performance. Commit to reviewing performance data regularly, drawing insights that guide better execution and sharper strategy.

DRAFTING MY GOVERANANCE PLAN
Is My Company Headed In the Right Direction?

A powerful governance plan crystallizes decision rights, cultural guardrails, and performance disciplines into a growth-propelling system. An effective Governance Plan galvanizes alignment, fuels accountability and propels strategic focus, ensuring every resource and action compounds toward your vision.

Outline a decisive and vision-aligned governance plan by answering these four guiding questions:

What is the core vision that anchors your business direction?
Define your vision and establish consistent communication channels to align your team and stakeholders.

Where will you concentrate your limited time and resources for maximum impact?
Identify key strategic priorities and create systems to minimize distractions and maintain focus.

What recurring workflows and responsibilities drive your business engine?
Map out essential business activities and streamline processes by assigning clear accountability and ownership.

What key metrics define success in your business?
Choose the leading indicators of success and set up real-time reviews, accountability and tools to drive performance and focus.

DRAFTING MY GOVERANANCE PLAN

Capture the quintessence of how your organization will govern its overall direction. Pursue discipline, intentional structure and adaptive leadership as you establish systems that align actions with enterprise-wide purpose.

Use the space below to architect your governance plan, detailing operational frameworks, strategic alignment tools and accountability mechanisms. Employ clear structure, actionable detail and confident foresight to build a business model capable of sustaining long-term success.

MY GOVERANANCE PLAN DRAFT:

This is your space to structure, refine and align the systems that will guide your company with clarity, responsibility and long-term integrity.

MONITORING YOUR COMMUNICATIONS
Are You Getting Your Brand Message Across?

🔒 KEY TACTICS

Describe My Manufacturing Process

How Are Your Goods Being Produced?

Identify how your products are made, from sourcing
raw materials to production and packaging.

Describe My Business Location

Where Are The Best Locations For Commerce?

Identify your business location and assess how it impacts
accessibility, logistics and customer relationships.

Describe My Brand Story

Does Your Brand Reflect the Heart of Your Business?

Identify the core message behind your brand - what it stands for,
why it exists and how it emotionally connects with your audience.

Describe My Supply Chain

How Will You Deliver Your Products/Services?

Identify and map out each stage of your supply chain ecosystem, from
sourcing materials to product delivery.

By *Monitoring Your Communications*, you guarantee every message
not only reaches its intended audience but truly engages - delivering clarity,
consistency, relevance and measurable impact across all channels, platforms and
interactions - online and in real life.

DESCRIBE MY MANUFACTURING PROCESS
How Are Your Goods Being Produced?

Right now: You are identifying how your products are made, from sourcing raw materials to production and packaging.

Recognize that: Your Manufacturing Process serves as the rigorous foundation for product excellence and operational precision. Describing each critical phase - from sourcing to assembly - ensures quality control, waste reduction and scalable production - regardless of demand fluctuations.

Outline: Start by detailing each stage of your production process with exact equipment, labor and cycle time requirements. Execute stringent quality checkpoints at critical phases to prevent defects, minimize waste and ensure consistent output that meets customer specifications.

DESCRIBE MY BUSINESS LOCATION
Where Are The Best Locations For Commerce?

Right now: You are identifying your business location and assess how it impacts accessibility, logistics and customer relationships.

KEY TAKEAWAY

Recognize that: Your Business Location serves as a pivotal asset shaping accessibility, efficiency and brand identity. Strategizing this presence - both physical or digital - ensures competitive advantage, customer convenience and operational resilience in evolving markets.

KEY ACTION

Outline: Start by detailing your current location's logistics efficiency, customer accessibility, and market penetration potential. Execute a brand-alignment audit to ensure your address reinforces professional credibility, meets operational demands and aligns with target customer expectations.

KEY NOTES

DESCRIBE MY BRAND STORY
Does Your Brand Reflect the Heart of Your Business?

Right now: You are identifying the core message behind your brand - what it stands for, why it exists and how it emotionally connects with your audience.

KEY TAKEAWAY

Recognize that: Your Brand Story serves as the authentic heartbeat of your business, forging emotional connections and competitive distinction. Crafting this narrative - through origins, values and purpose - ensures memorability, customer loyalty and market differentiation.

KEY ACTION

Outline: Start by detailing the core elements of your brand's journey: the inspiration behind its inception, the problems it solves and the values it upholds. Execute on narrative training for all teams to ensure every product description, advertisement and service interaction radiates your purpose.

KEY NOTES

DESCRIBE MY SUPPLY CHAIN
How Will You Deliver Your Products/Services?

Right now: You are identifying each stage of your supply chain, from sourcing materials to product delivery, and assess its reliability, cost-efficiency and scalability.

🔷 KEY TAKEAWAY

Recognize that: Your Supply Chain serves as the precision-engineered backbone of product excellence and operational reliability. Describing its nodes and flows from suppliers to warehouses to transport - prevents bottlenecks, ensures accountability and delivers consistent value.

🔓 KEY ACTION

Outline: Start by detailing each stage of your supply chain process, including suppliers, manufacturers, logistics providers and distribution channels. Execute on opportunities to streamline logistics, enhance supplier relationships and build systems that can adapt to disruptions and growth.

✏️ KEY NOTES

DRAFTING MY COMMUNICATIONS PLAN
Are We Getting Our Brand Message Across?

A powerful communications plan crystallizes your core narratives, audience psychology, and channel strategies into a perception-shaping force. An effective Communications Plan galvanizes attention, fuels engagement and propels action, ensuring every message and medium advances your strategic objectives with precision.

Outline a compelling and results-driven communications plan by answering these four guiding questions:

How does your manufacturing reinforce your brand promise?
Design production with intentional differentiators then showcase these proof points to justify premium positioning.

How can your physical or digital footprint actively enhance your brand story and customer experience?
Evaluate how your workspace shapes customer perception and employee culture and optimize it accordingly.

How does your inventory strategy support your brand promises?
Align your stock levels and turnover with customer expectations using real-time data for availability, quality and reliability.

How transparent, ethical and efficient is your supply chain?
Promote supply chain practices that reflect your brand's commitment to ethics, transparency and operational excellence.

DRAFTING MY COMMUNICATIONS PLAN

Capture the quintessence of how your business communicates its values, message and identity. Pursue clarity, consistency and audience connection as you design systems that reinforce your branding across every channel.

Use the space below to architect your communications plan, mapping out messaging strategies, alignment opportunities and transparency goals. Employ actionable tactics, compelling language and adaptive frameworks to build a communication model that deepens trust and drives engagement.

MY COMMUNICATIONS PLAN DRAFT:

This is your space to shape, refine and align your communication systems for clarity, consistency and connection.

©

CONTROL YOUR FINANCES
Are You Watching Your Budgets & Investments?

Supervise My Cash Flow

What Are Your Company's Sources of Income?

Identify how and where your company's sales revenues are being generated, pinpointed by product, channel and customer segment.

Supervise My Investments

What Are Your Startup and Business Operating Costs?

Identify all of the costs associated with launching and running your business enterprise.

Supervise My Net Worth

What Is The Financial Value of Your Business?

Identify the total value of all your business assets after subtracting your total business liabilities.

Supervise My Profit Margins

How Much Profit Is Your Company Generating?

Identify the difference between your company's revenue against direct and indirect costs to determine the profitability of your business.

By ***Controlling Your Finances*** with expert oversight, you command every dollar's complete journey—meticulously tracing transaction origins in real-time, intelligently mastering cash flow dynamics, strategically optimizing operational expenditures and systematically fortifying your financial future.

SUPERVISE MY CASH FLOW

What Are Your Company's Sources of Income?

Right now: You are identifying how and where your company's sales revenues are being generated, pinpointed by product, channel and customer segment.

KEY TAKEAWAY

Recognize that: Your Cash Flow serves as the central nervous system of business operations, dictating daily liquidity and strategic agility. Supervising these financial rhythms ensures working capital resilience, risk mitigation and data-driven allocation of resources for maximum growth impact.

KEY ACTION

Outline: Start by listing all primary and secondary income sources, such as direct product or service sales, subscription fees, licensing agreements and affiliate commissions. Execute monthly volatility analyses to optimize high-margin channels and mitigate reliance on unpredictable income sources.

KEY NOTES

SUPERVISE MY EXPENSES

How Will You Monitor and Manage Company Expenditures?

Right now: You are identifying all of the investments and costs associated with launching and running your business enterprise.

Recognize that: Your Operating Expenses serve as the precision calibration point between fiscal discipline and innovation investment. Supervising these outlays optimizes return-on-investment (ROI), eliminates waste and reallocates capital to high-impact initiatives that accelerate market leadership.

Outline: Start by identifying key expense categories such as rent, utilities, payroll, marketing and professional services into fixed and variable costs. Execute monthly audits to cut waste, prioritize essential spending and reallocate budgets to match current business priorities.

SUPERVISE MY NET WORTH

What Is the Financial Value of Your Business Today?

Right now: You are identifying the total value of all your business assets after subtracting your total business liabilities.

KEY TAKEAWAY

Recognize that: Your Net Worth serves as the definitive scorecard of accumulated value and financial resilience. Supervising this metric tracks asset performance, debt efficiency and equity growth to inform strategic pivots and strengthen stakeholder confidence.

KEY ACTION

Outline: Start by inventorying all tangible and intangible assets, such as cash, equipment, inventory, and intellectual property. Then, subtract liabilities including loans, accounts payable and other debts to determine your real net worth. Execute quarterly net worth calculations to track your financial health.

KEY NOTES

SUPERVISE MY MARGINS

How Much Profit Is Your Company Generating?

Right now: You are identifying the difference between your company's revenue against direct and indirect costs to determine the profitability of your business.

Recognize that: Your Profit Margins serve as the ultimate barometer of pricing strategy efficiency and sustainable value creation. Supervising these ratios safeguards competitive positioning, exposes cost leaks and identifies reinvestment opportunities to compound long-term scalability.

Outline: Start by benchmarching your gross/operating/net margins against industry peers. Execute quarterly deep-dives to explain variances, spotlight competitive advantages and justify strategic reinvestment or cost-cutting measures to stakeholders.

DRAFTING MY FINANCIAL PLAN
Am I Watching My Budgets & Investments?

A powerful financial controls framework crystallizes cash flow discipline, margin mastery and risk mitigation into a profit-engineering engine. An effective control system galvanizes fiscal vigilance, fuels strategic reinvestment and propels sustainable growth - ensuring every dollar compounds toward enterprise dominance.

Outline a rigorous and profit-engineering financial controls plan by answering these four guiding questions:

How are you tracking cash inflows and outflows to ensure liquidity and day-to-day operational stability?
Implement regular cash flow monitoring using rolling forecasts and real-time tracking tools to maintain sufficient liquidity.

Are your expenses aligned with strategic priorities and expected returns?
Establish budgeting controls and approval processes to monitor spending and ensure alignment with your financial goals.

How are you regularly assessing your company's financial position through balance sheet metrics?
Conduct periodic balance sheet reviews to evaluate assets, liabilities and net worth, supporting informed decision-making.

How are you calculating, tracking and optimizing your profit margins across products or services?
Use detailed margin analysis and regular performance reviews to identify opportunities for cost reduction and margin improvement.

DRAFTING MY FINANCIAL PLAN

Capture the quintessence of how your business manages its financial health through disciplined oversight. Pursue precision, fiscal responsibility and long-term resilience as you design systems that ensure profitability.

Use the space below to architect your financial controls plan, outlining monitoring mechanisms, budget adherence strategies and fiscal policies. Employ actionable safeguards, rigorous tracking tools and adaptive practices to build a financial discipline framework..

MY FINANCIAL CONTROLS DRAFT:

This is your space to design, refine and strengthen the financial safeguards that will protect and empower your business.

GLOSSARY OF ENTREPRENEURIAL TERMS
Words shape reality. Speak with wisdom. Build with care.

Accounting
The disciplined system for tracking, analyzing and reporting financial transactions to understand the health and performance of your business. Accounting gives structure to your company's past, present and future numbers.

Advertising
The strategic use of paid media—including print, radio, digital, and broadcast—to capture public attention, spark desire, and direct it toward your brand.

Angel Investors
Private individuals who believe in your vision and invest capital in exchange for equity. Often the first believers outside your circle.

Assets
Everything your business owns that holds value—from cash and equipment to intellectual property and brand equity.

Balance Sheet
A financial snapshot capturing a company's assets, liabilities, and equity at a specific moment in time. A mirror of your business's standing.

Brand
The soul of your company made visible. It's your identity, your voice, your vibe—and how the world perceives your presence.

Brand Loyalty
The emotional commitment of customers who choose your brand over and over, not just for the product, but for the experience.

Break-Even Point

The moment when your total revenue covers your total expenses—when your business crosses from red to black.

Business Concept

The original spark. A concise explanation of your Big Idea, what it offers, who it serves and how it stands out.

Business Model

The system through which your company creates, delivers, and captures value. The economic engine of your enterprise.

Business Plan

A detailed roadmap that translates your vision into strategy, structure, and steps. The written spell that brings your dream to life.

Capital

The financial resources—cash, credit or assets—used to fund your operations, expansion and evolution.

Cash Flow Statement

A vital financial report that tracks how cash enters and exits your business, helping you stay liquid and responsive.

Company Vision

The future you are building. Your business's highest goal—the why behind the work and the dream behind the drive.

Competitive Advantage

What makes your company superior in the marketplace. It's your edge, your distinction, your unfair advantage.

Core Values

The non-negotiable truths that guide your decisions and shape your culture. Your business's moral compass.

Cost of Goods Sold (COGS)

The direct costs associated with producing your product or service, including materials, labor and manufacturing.

Corporation
A separate legal entity owned by shareholders, offering liability protection and tax advantages.

Customer Acquisition Cost (CAC)
The total expense required to gain a new customer, including marketing, sales,and outreach.

Customer Journey
The experience a customer has with your brand—from first awareness to long-term loyalty.

Demographics
The quantifiable characteristics of your market—such as age, income, education, and lifestyle—that inform your marketing decisions.

Demand
The market's desire for your product at a given time and price. A core driver of pricing, production and planning.

Distribution Channels
The pathways through which your products reach your customers—retail, wholesale, direct-to-consumer or digital.

Elevator Pitch
A concise, compelling summary of your Big Idea, designed to captivate in 30 seconds or less.

Entrepreneur
A visionary who transforms ideas into action, embracing both risk and reward in the pursuit of freedom, impact and innovation.

Financial Budget
A forward-looking financial map forecasting income, expenses, and profitability over a defined period.

Financial Plan
The strategic framework that defines how you will generate revenue, control costs, fund growth and remain profitable.

Freedom

The power to design your own destiny. Entrepreneurship's ultimate promise and greatest reward.

Income Statement

A financial report that reveals a company's performance by showing revenue, expenses and net profit over time.

Income Taxes

The portion of your earnings paid to federal, state and local governments based on your net income.

Industry Trends

The shifts and movements defining your market's direction—key to staying relevant, responsive and innovative.

Intellectual Property (IP)

Creations of the mind—such as trademarks, copyrights, patents, and trade secrets—that offer exclusive rights and value to your brand.

Inventory

The physical goods or raw materials you hold for sale or production. A balancing act between supply and demand.

Joint Venture

A formal partnership between two or more entities to pursue a shared goal, often for a limited time or specific project.

Key Performance Indicators (KPIs)

Quantifiable measures of success. These metrics track progress toward your goals and spotlight what's working—or not.

Liabilities

The debts, obligations and financial responsibilities owed to others. A key part of your business's financial equation.

Limited Liability Company (LLC)

A flexible business structure that protects personal assets while providing tax benefits and operational simplicity.

Logo
The visual symbol of your brand—designed to be instantly recognizable and emotionally resonant.

Market
The collective group of potential customers your product or service is designed to serve.

Market Price
The current value your product commands in the open market—shaped by supply, demand and perception.

Market Research
The process of gathering insight into customer needs, competitor offerings and overall industry conditions.

Marketing Plan
A strategic document outlining how you will reach, attract, convert and retain customers through messaging, media and action.

Merchandising
The art of displaying and promoting products in a way that maximizes sales appeal and reinforces brand identity.

Mergers
The combination of two or more companies into one, often to gain market share, efficiency or competitive strength.

Mission Statement
A succinct expression of your company's purpose, values and impact—your reason for being.

Minimum Viable Product (MVP)
The most basic version of your product that can be released to early users to validate assumptions and gather feedback.

Networking
The intentional practice of building connections, relationships and collaborations that advance your business goals.

Net Worth
The value of your business calculated as total assets minus total liabilities. Your equity, your foundation.

Operating Expenses
The ongoing costs necessary to run your business—rent, salaries, utilities and day-to-day essentials.

Operations
The systems, processes, and workflows that turn your mission into motion and your strategy into results.

Partnership
A business entity owned by two or more people who share in profits, losses and decision-making responsibilities.

Press Kit
A curated collection of brand materials—bios, images, press releases and company facts—designed to inform media and spark publicity.

Pricing
The strategy and science of setting a value for your offerings that balances cost, demand, perception and profit.

Profits
The financial reward of your entrepreneurial efforts—what remains after all expenses have been covered.

Public Relations (PR)
The art of shaping public perception through storytelling, media engagement and relationship-building.

Publicity
Organic, often free media exposure generated through buzz, events, announcements or coverage.

Return on Investment (ROI)
A measure of the efficiency and profitability of an investment - calculated as net gain divided by cost.

Revenues

The total income generated from business activities before expenses are deducted.

Risk

The potential for loss, uncertainty, or failure. The price of admission for entrepreneurship—and the crucible for reward.

Sales

The exchange of goods or services for money. The fuel that powers business momentum.

Sales Funnel

The customer journey—from awareness to action—mapped out as stages that convert interest into revenue.

Sales Promotions

Short-term tactics and incentives designed to boost visibility, engagement and sales.

Scalability

The ability of your business model and operations to grow efficiently without proportionally increasing costs.

Sole Proprietorship

A simple business structure with one owner who assumes full responsibility for operations, liabilities and profits.

Startup Capital

The initial funds required to launch your venture—often covering product development, marketing and operations.

Strategic Alliance

A long-term collaboration between organizations that share resources, expertise and market access for mutual benefit.

Supply

The quantity of a product or service available for purchase at a given time and price.

Taxes

Mandatory financial charges imposed by governments on your income, property and transactions.

Traction

Evidence that your business model is working—measured by growth, engagement, revenue or user adoption.

Unique Selling Proposition (USP)

The distinct benefit or feature that makes your product the preferred choice over the competition.

Valuation

The financial worth of your business, based on assets, earnings, growth potential, and market factors.

Venture Capitalists (VCs)

Professional investors who provide capital to startups in exchange for equity, usually expecting high growth and returns.

Vision Statement

A bold and inspiring declaration of your company's future impact and ideal destination.